E. Schubert, Nautical Almanac Office

Tables of Eunomia

E. Schubert, Nautical Almanac Office

Tables of Eunomia

ISBN/EAN: 9783742889416

Manufactured in Europe, USA, Canada, Australia, Japa

Cover: Foto ©Andreas Hilbeck / pixelio.de

Manufactured and distributed by brebook publishing software
(www.brebook.com)

E. Schubert, Nautical Almanac Office

Tables of Eunomia

TABLES

OF

EUNOMIA,

BY

E. SCHUBERT

COMPUTED FOR THE

AMERICAN EPHEMERIS AND NAUTICAL ALMANAC.

BUREAU OF NAVIGATION,
WASHINGTON.
1866.

INTRODUCTION.

THE general perturbations of Eunomia having been computed exactly in the same manner as those of Melpomene, it is only necessary to refer here to the Melpomene-Tables for details, and to give the data which have been used in the computation with the final results thereof.

Elements.

EUNOMIA.		**JUPITER (from BOUVARD's Tables).**	
1854, Jan. 0, Washington Mean Time; (osculating).		1854, Jan. 0, Washington Mean Time.	

Eunomia:
$$M = 122°\ 10'\ 34".2$$
$$n = 27\ 47\ 12.1$$
$$\Omega = 293\ 55\ 42.0 \left.\right\} \text{M. Eq. Ep.}$$
$$i = 11\ 44\ 5.2$$
$$\varphi = 10\ 50\ 11.9$$
$$\mu = 825".79753$$
$$\log a = 0.4220887$$

Jupiter (from Bouvard's Tables):
$$M = 269°\ 43'\ 39".1$$
$$n = 11\ 58\ 43.2$$
$$\Omega = 98\ 56\ 38.7 \left.\right\} \text{M. Eq. Ep.}$$
$$i = 1\ 18\ 39.5$$
$$\varphi = 2\ 45\ 55.1$$
$$\mu = 299".12861$$
$$\log a = 0.7162370$$

Perturbations of the Radius Vector in units of the Sixth Decimal Place.

							$r°\ \delta r$					
i, i'	cos	sin	i, i'	cos	sin	i, i'	cos	sin	i, i'	cos	sin
0 0	− 7.74		−4 −2	− 0.2	0.0	1 −4	+ 28.6	+ 49.1	−1 −7	− 0.3	− 0.2
1 0	+ 27.09	− 444.62	−3 −2	+ 3.0	− 2.5	2 −4	− 104.4	− 56.1	0 −7	+ 1.1	− 0.7
2 0	+ 2.52	− 41.49	−2 −2	+ 19.2	− 13.0	3 −4	+ 86.7	− 446.1	1 −7	+ 8.5	+ 3.3
3 0	+ 0.35	− 5.80	−1 −2	+ 136.2	− 93.5	4 −4	− 60.4	+ 95.8	2 −7	+ 15.8	+ 11.6
4 0	+ 0.06	− 0.96	0 −2	+1869.2	−1287.5	5 −4	− 11.7	+ 19.9	3 −7	+ 23.8	− 21.6
5 0	+ 0.01	− 0.18	1 −2	−1693.1	+1184.4	6 −4	− 1.9	+ 2.1	4 −7	− 11.9	− 12.2
6 0		− 0.03	2 −2	−6071.2	+3841.8	7 −4	− 0.2	− 0.1	5 −7	+ 10.2	+ 3.2
			3 −2	− 565.8	+ 360.1				6 −7	− 4.1	7.0
0 0	+ 549.2		4 −2	− 74.7	+ 45.5	−2 −5	+ 0.4	+ 0.5	7 −7	− 0.2	+ 2.5
1 0	− 157.8	− 8.5	5 −2	− 12.2	+ 7.0	−1 −5	+ 1.2	+ 2.0	8 −7	+ 0.4	+ 1.7
2 0	+ 23.2	− 12.3	6 −2	− 1.4	+ 1.0	0 −5	− 3.1	+ 12.9	9 −7	+ 0.3	+ 0.4
3 0	+ 1.1	− 2.4	7 −2	0.0	+ 0.1	1 −5	− 45.6	+ 65.4			
4 . 0	+ 0.4	− 0.1				2 −5	+ 41.5	− 71.6	−1 −8	+ 0.1	0.0
5 0	0.0	+ 0.3	−4 −3	+ 0.3	0.0	3 −5	+ 226.2	+ 142.2	0 −8	+ 0.8	− 0.2
6 0	− 0.2	0.0	−3 −3	+ 2.0	+ 0.3	4 −5	+ 18.1	− 81.1	1 −8	+ 3.3	+ 0.1
7 0	0.0	− 0.2	−2 −3	+ 8.1	+ 1.1	5 −5	− 7.5	+ 34.0	2 −8	+ 31.5	− 14.9
			−1 −3	+ 57.7	− 2.6	6 −5	− 2.1	+ 9.0	3 −8	− 17.4	+ 11.1
−5 −1	+ 0.4	+ 0.1	0 −3	+ 621.4	− 4.3	7 −5	+ 0.1	+ 1.2	4 −8	+ 2.7	+ 6.7
−4 −1	− 0.2	+ 0.6	1 −3	+1215.8	−1375.0	8 −5	0.0	+ 0.4	5 −8	− 2.7	+ 1.7
−3 −1	− 1.5	+ 0.2	2 −3	−3385.9	+4687.3				6 −8	+ 3.8	+ 1.4
−2 −1	− 0.1	+ 2.7	3 −3	− 781.8	+ 958.8	−2 −6	+ 0.3	0.0	7 −8	− 2.6	− 3.3
−1 −1	+ 58.7	+ 41.6	4 −3	− 102.2	+ 123.3	−1 −6	− 0.3	+ 0.5	8 −8	+ 0.5	+ 0.8
0 −1	− 731.7	+ 245.2	5 −3	− 12.9	+ 16.5	0 −6	− 3.5	− 0.9	9 −8	0.0	+ 0.6
1 −1	+1802.6	− 579.8	6 −3	− 2.2	+ 3.1	1 −6	− 16.9	− 15.1			
2 −1	+ 343.0	− 110.5	7 −3	− 0.5	+ 0.2	2 −6	− 26.1	+ 26.3			
3 −1	+ 59.4	− 21.4	8 −3	− 0.1	− 0.2	3 −6	+ 51.2	− 64.0			
4 −1	+ 8.5	− 2.1				4 −6	+ 24.5	+ 15.1			
5 −1	+ 0.7	− 0.3	−2 −4	− 0.4	0.0	5 −6	− 6.1	− 28.8			
6 −1	0.0	− 0.4	−1 −4	+ 0.5	− 1.6	6 −6	+ 0.4	+ 9.8			
7 −1	+ 0.2	− 0.1	0 −4	+ 7.8	− 2.8	7 −6	0.0	+ 4.1			
						8 −6	0.0	+ 0.9			

Denoting now the Arguments in the following manner: —

I =	— M'	XVIII =	2 M — 5 M'	XXXV =	7 M — 3 M'
II =	M — M'	XIX =	M — 5 M'	XXXVI =	5 M — 6 M'
III =	M — 2 M'	XX =	3 M — 5 M'	XXXVII = —	M — 5 M'
IV =	M — 3 M'	XXI =	5 M — 3 M'	XXXVIII = —	3 M — M'
V =	3 M — 2 M'	XXII =	5 M — 2 M'	XXXIX =	7 M — 2 M'
VI =	2 M — 3 M'	XXIII = —	2 M — 3 M'	XL =	5 M — 7 M'
VII =	2 M — M'	XXIV =	4 M — 5 M'	XLI =	5 M — 8 M'
VIII = —	M — M'	XXV =	M — 6 M'	XLII =	6 M — M'
IX =	M	XXVI =	2 M — 7 M'	XLIII = —	4 M — 3 M'
X =	3 M — M'	XXVII = —	3 M — 2 M'	XLIV =	6 M — 5 M'
XI =	M — 4 M'	XXVIII =	3 M — 7 M'	XLV = —	M — 4 M'
XII =	3 M — 4 M'	XXIX =	3 M — 8 M'	XLVI =	6 M — 7 M'
XIII = —	2 M — M'	XXX =	4 M — 7 M'	XLVII =	8 M — 3 M'
XIV =	4 M — M'	XXXI =	5 M — M'	XLVIII = —	2 M — 5 M'
XV = —	M — 2 M'	XXXII =	M — 8 M'	XLIX = —	M — 6 M'
XVI =	4 M — 3 M'	XXXIII =	5 M — 4 M'		
XVII = —	M — 3 M'	XXXIV =	M — 7 M'		

The perturbations of the rectangular coördinates (the plane of the orbit of Eunomia being fundamental-plane) in units of the Sixth Decimal, are: —

	ξ_1		η_1		ζ_1	
	cos	sin	cos	sin	cos	sin
0 M	+ 15.58t		− 88.02t		+ 3.08t	
1 M	+ 1.42t	+581.71t	−570.90t	+ 2.41t	− 10.77t	−154.18t
2 M	− 4.83t	+136.55t	−135.37t	− 4.61t	− 1.00t	− 14.39t
3 M	− 1.37t	+ 30.59t	− 30.40t	− 1.32t	− 0.14t	− 2.01t
4 M	− 0.34t	+ 6.97t	− 6.92t	− 0.33t	0.00	− 0.33t
5 M	− 0.09t	+ 1.61t	− 1.60t	− 0.08t	0.00	− 0.08t
6 M	0.00	+ 0.38t	− 0.36t	0.00	0.00	0.00
7 M	0.00	+ 0.07t	− 0.07t	0.00	0.00	0.00
I	+1370.2	− 403.1	− 407.0	−1232.5	− 181.1	+ 44.9
2 I	−4033.9	+2671.0	+2648.5	+4008.6	+ 190.7	− 114.2
3 I	−1277.4	+ 153.2	+ 157.7	+1263.9	+ 6.7	− 56.1
4 I	− 9.3	− 7.1	− 6.2	+ 8.8	+ 1.0	+ 0.9
5 I	+ 18.2	− 16.2	− 16.4	− 16.9		
6 I	+ 6.0	− 2.4	0.0	− 6.0		
7 I	− 2.2	− 1.0	− 0.9	+ 1.8		
8 I	− 2.0	+ 0.9	+ 1.1	+ 2.0		
II	− 79.4	+ 59.7	− 54.5	− 53.4	+ 172.9	− 53.9
2 II	+2665.1	−1775.8	+1690.3	+2529.3	− 123.7	+ 84.1
3 II	+ 807.8	− 982.8	+ 973.8	+ 806.0	− 54.6	+ 59.5
4 II	− 3.2	+ 58.1	− 46.8	+ 2.1	+ 1.7	− 1.7
5 II	− 13.1	+ 3.0	+ 2.2	− 11.7		
6 II	− 0.7	+ 2.0	0.0	− 0.9		
7 II	0.0	+ 1.2	0.0	0.0		

	ξ_1		η_1		ζ_1	
	cos	sin	cos	sin	cos	sin
III	−2487.1	+1518.2	+1488.7	+2339.3	− 193.2	+ 101.9
2 III	+ 40.9	− 197.9	− 158.9	− 41.4	0.0	− 27.0
3 III	+ 9.6	+ 11.4	+ 1.8	− 37.0	+ 7.9	+ 2.1
4 III	+ 21.3	− 17.0	+ 19.1	+ 23.0	− 0.6	0.0
IV	−1695.2	+2903.8	+2902.8	+1721.5	+ 162.9	− 164.6
2 IV	+ 13.2	− 32.5	− 25.2	− 26.9	− 2.6	− 0.6
V	+1202.5	− 774.7	+ 760.0	+1181.9	− 1.5	0.0
2 V	+ 1.0	+ 1.4	− 1.6	+ 1.0		
VI	+1055.0	+ 366.0	− 117.0	+1341.5	− 507.5	+ 518.5
2 VI	− 14.0	+ 6.0	− 26.2	− 10.4	+ 2.6	+ 5.8
VII	− 634.8	+ 200.6	− 204.2	− 640.0	+ 79.9	− 29.1
2 VII	+ 319.8	− 204.8	+ 202.7	+ 317.1		
3 VII	+ 15.4	− 19.8	+ 19.5	+ 15.4		
VIII	+ 235.1	− 96.1	− 94.2	− 238.4	− 63.1	+ 20.9
2 VIII	− 116.2	+ 80.4	+ 80.5	+ 115.8	+ 2.5	− 1.7
3 VIII	− 11.7	+ 0.8	+ 1.2	+ 15.9		
0 IX	− 69.2		− 14.1		+ 72.3	
1 IX	+ 193.5	+ 1.1	+ 2.2	+ 172.2	− 51.2	+ 4.3
2 IX	+ 51.6	+ 8.1	− 7.7	+ 53.6	− 12.1	
3 IX	+ 6.6	+ 2.4	− 1.0	+ 6.8	− 2.0	
4 IX	+ 0.7	+ 0.6		+ 0.8		
X	− 158.3	+ 50.7	− 49.8	− 157.6	+ 7.9	− 3.1
2 X	+ 20.2	− 12.9	+ 11.8	+ 18.4		
XI	− 60.4	− 139.4	− 137.9	+ 64.1	+ 0.5	+ 16.4
2 XI	− 23.3	+ 19.7	+ 17.8	+ 22.4		
XII	+ 5.5	+ 117.3	+ 6.2	+ 64.6	+ 22.8	− 45.4
2 XII	− 0.7	− 1.4	− 1.2	+ 1.8		
XIII	+ 29.3	− 19.6	− 19.3	− 30.6	− 7.6	+ 2.0
2 XIII	− 6.0	+ 4.1	+ 4.2	+ 6.3		
XIV	− 38.0	+ 12.4	− 12.2	− 37.4	+ 0.9	0.0
2 XIV	+ 1.2	− 0.7	+ 0.7	+ 1.2		
XV	− 600.9	+ 415.0	+ 412.6	+ 599.3	+ 17.2	− 12.3
XVI	+ 238.8	− 305.9	+ 301.0	+ 235.3	− 5.0	+ 4.9
XVII	− 251.6	+ 19.8	+ 18.9	+ 250.1	+ 1.3	− 5.7
XVIII	+ 109.7	+ 101.8	+ 36.0	− 57.1	+ 2.6	− 10.6
XIX	+ 172.1	− 21.8	− 24.5	− 174.0	− 3.9	0.0
XX	− 128.8	−. 9.1	− 64.9	− 118.7	+ 4.1	+ 46.0
XXI	+ 61.7	− 79.5	+ 79.1	+ 61.1	− 0.8	+ 0.7
XXII	+ 78.9	− 50.3	+ 50.3	+ 78.8		
XXIII	− 53.3	+ 3.8	+ 3.7	+ 53.9	0.0	− 0.8
XXIV	− 53.1	+ 2.8	+ 32.0	− 44.0	+ 2.3	− 5.1
XXV	+ 26.9	− 53.6	− 11.2	− 28.2		

	$\mathfrak{S}_1$		η_1		ζ_1	
	cos	sin	cos	sin	cos	sin
XXVI	+ 28.9	− 17.9	− 20.7	− 26.4		
XXVII	− 24.7	+ 17.1	+ 17.1	+ 24.8		
XXVIII	+ 14.1	− 2.3	− 2.9	+ 31.7		
XXIX	+ 18.9	− 11.1	− 5.3	+ 5.2		
XXX	− 9.5	+ 11.5	− 8.9	− 18.0		
XXXI	− 9.1	+ 2.9	− 3.2	− 9.4		
XXXII	− 8.4	+ 4.4	+ 4.5	+ 8.6		
XXXIII	+ 1.9	+ 9.9	− 9.8	+ 2.2	. . .	− 1.4
XXXIV	− 7.0	− 2.4	− 1.3	+ 7.1		
XXXV	+ 3.6	− 4.9	+ 4.6	+ 3.5		
XXXVI	− 4.1	+ 7.6	+ 2.9	− 5.2	. . .	− 2.0
XXXVII	+ 3.1	− 4.6	− 3.9	− 3.1		
XXXVIII	+ 4.2	− 4.0	− 4.5	− 4.4	− 1.0	
XXXIX	+ 4.4	− 2.8	+ 2.7	+ 4.3		
XL	− 3.1	0.0	− 5.7	+ 1.1	+ 0.6	+ 1.3
XLI	+ 3.9	− 0.8	+ 1.2	+ 0.9		
XLII	− 2.2	+ 0.7	− 0.7	− 4.3		
XLIII	− 2.6	0.0	0.0	+ 2.4		
XLIV	− 2.8	− 0.6	+ 0.9	− 2.9		
XLV	− 2.1	− 0.7	− 0.8	+ 1.7		
XLVI	− 0.5	+ 2.1	+ 1.2	− 0.9		
XLVII	+ 0.8	− 1.0	+ 1.0	+ 0.7		
XLVIII	+ 0.5	− 1.3	− 1.1	− 1.0		
XLIX	+ 1.5	0.0	0.0	− 1.2		

Normal Places referred to the Mean Equinox 1854.0.

Berlin M. T.		α	δ	Berlin M. T.		α	δ
1851 August	20.5	271 57 19.76	− 24 27 41.23	1856 October	15.5	10 36 41.36	+ 28 2 54.83
1852 January	3.5	313 46 58.27	− 12 41 35.93	1858 February	25.5	152 28 4.57	− 1 26 19.94
1852 July	19.5	49 6 27.33	+ 28 59 10.56	1859 May	24.5	219 25 28.73	− 31 21 19.01
1853 January	8.5	66 35 15.96	+ 30 46 35.07	1860 August	24.5	325 45 51.73	− 0 49 25.31
1854 March	13.5	174 6 44.57	− 14 27 46.74				

By means of which and the above perturbations were obtained for a first approximation:—

$$\delta M = -1'\ 31''.2 \qquad \delta\varphi = -2'\ 39''.3 \qquad \delta\pi = +4'\ 44''.9 \qquad \delta\Omega = -3'\ 34''.4$$
$$\delta i = +11''.9 \qquad \delta\mu = -0''.34332$$

and by adding these corrections to the elements from which we have started we get the corrected elliptical elements:—

1854.0, Washington Mean Time.

$$M\ 122\overset{\circ}{\ }\ 9'\ 3''.0$$
$$\pi\ \ 27\ 51\ 57.0\ \Big\}\ \text{M. Eq. Eps.}$$
$$\Omega\ \ 293\ 52\ 7.6\ \Big/$$
$$i\ \ 11\ 44\ 17.1$$
$$\varphi\ \ 10\ 47\ 32.6$$
$$\mu\ \ 825''.45421$$
$$\log a\quad 0.4222090$$

In order to neglect nothing these elements were corrected once more. The equations of condition from the second computation of the normals and the differential-coefficients are:—

δM	$\delta\varphi$	$\delta\pi$	$\delta\Omega$	δi	$100\,\delta\mu$	
+1.1641	-2.4611	+1.2622	+0.0378	+0.0167	-10.9529	- 8.81
+0.7803	-1.2054	+0.6465	+0.0456	-0.1779	- 5.9148	- 1.35
+1.1872	+0.4821	+0.7994	-0.0185	-0.1462	- 5.6645	+ 2.34
+2.0201	+2.4619	+1.5174	-0.0391	-0.0107	- 7.9145	- 1.79
+0.9476	+1.1690	+1.2832	+0.0326	-0.6368	+ 0.6934	+ 8.55
+2.4555	-0.5757	+1.6567	-0.0534	-0.7658	+24.7850	+16.76
+1.0839	+1.9946	+1.3062	+0.0871	-0.5068	+16.3537	-14.56
+1.0058	-0.9330	+1.4029	-0.0617	-0.3101	+19.5445	+ 9.64
+1.9221	-2.8205	+1.5224	+0.1120	-0.5060	+46.5036	-10.68
+0.2872	-0.5734	+0.2883	-0.2788	-0.0807	- 2.5003	+ 4.20
+0.4088	-0.6695	+0.3380	-0.1258	+0.3468	- 3.0799	+ 0.15
+0.1957	+0.0852	+0.1318	+0.0118	+0.8800	- 0.9257	+ 0.39
+0.0327	+0.0568	+0.0273	+0.2793	+0.7637	- 0.0953	+ 1.68
-0.5050	-0.5362	-0.7003	+0.1250	-1.1525	- 0.6020	- 7.66
+1.1626	+0.1397	+0.7786	-0.0262	+1.6109	+12.3054	+ 5.37
-0.6061	-1.0770	-0.7511	+0.2079	-0.8779	- 9.3529	+ 6.84
-0.2668	+0.3232	-0.3615	-0.1265	-1.2442	- 5.3754	- 1.14
+1.1118	-1.4654	+0.8526	-0.2561	+0.8961	+27.2230	- 7.34

$$=0$$

Final Equation.

+ 23.8806	- 3.9333	+ 20.0588	-0.4640	- 0.0002	+ 197.8080	+ 9.833	
- 3.9333	+ 33.0398	- 2.7307	+0.0269	+ 0.4937	- 143.9647	+ 18.077	
+ 20.0588 δM	- 2.7307 $\delta\varphi$	+ 18.0722 $\delta\pi$	-0.3962 $\delta\Omega$	- 0.0153 δi	+ 167.6261 $100\,\delta\mu$	+ 4.063	$=0$
- 0.4640	+ 0.0269	- 0.3962	+0.3461	- 0.3040	- 3.7281	- 2.412	
- 0.0002	+ 0.4937	- 0.0153	-0.3040	+10.1839	+ 2.5371	- 1.062	
+197.8080	-143.9647	+167.6261	-3.7291	+ 2.5371	+4702.3730	-218.109	

from which,

$$\delta M = -4''.00 \qquad \delta\varphi = -0''.38 \qquad \delta\pi = +3''.55 \qquad \delta\Omega = +6''.85$$
$$\delta i = +0''.31 \qquad \delta\mu = +0''.00082$$

so that we finally have the corrected elements for the construction of the Tables:—

1854.0, Washington Mean Time.

$$
\begin{aligned}
M\ & 122°\ 8'\ 58''.91 \\
n\ & 27\ 52\ 0.51 \\
\Omega\ & 293\ 52\ 14.49 \\
i\ & 11\ 44\ 17.36 \\
\varphi\ & 10\ 47\ 32.18 \\
\mu\ & 825''.45503 \\
\log a\ & 0.4222087
\end{aligned}
$$
M. Eq. Ep.

By these elements the normals are represented thus:—

$\Delta\,\alpha\cos\delta$	$\Delta\delta$	$\Delta\,\alpha\cos\delta$	$\Delta\delta$
-8.7	+2.2	+14.5	+4.8
-1.9	-1.0	-13.3	+7.4
-0.4	+0.3	+12.0	-3.2
-6.3	+3.8	- 7.5	-7.5
+9.0	-7.5		

The greater residuals are evidently the effect of the neglected perturbations by Saturn, so that the whole speaks well for the perturbations by Jupiter.

Example for computing a Place from the Tables.

1863, April $18^d.5$, Berlin M. T. = April 18^d 5^h 58^m 15^s Washington M. T.

log e	log $\frac{1-e}{1+e}$	log p
9.272419	9.835416	0.406708

We will refer the place to the apparent equinox. Precession from the beginning of the year up to April $18^d.5 = + 14''.93$; Nutation $= + 15''.28$; therefore Variation of $\Omega = + 30''.2$; Apparent Obliquity minus Mean Obliquity at the beginning of the year $= - 3''.1$.

		cos $(x_1 x)$	cos $(y_1 x)$	cos $(z_1 x)$	cos $(x_1 y)$	cos $(y_1 y)$
Table V.,	1863,	9.936487	9.670264n	9.269220n	9.534017	9.911812
Table VI.	$+ 30''.2$	−31.1	+120.8	−29.3	+148.9	−32.3
	$- 3''.1$				+6.2	− 4.0
		9.936456	9.670385n	9.269191n	9.534172	9.911784

		cos $(x_1 y)$	cos $(z_1 z)$	cos $(y_1 z)$	cos $(z_1 z)$
Table V.,	1863,	9.668033n	9.567775	9.529821	9.937137
Table VI.	$+ 30''.2$	+23.2	+59.5	−30.5	−5.1
	$- 3''.1$	−11.8	−6.2	−15.5	+3.1
		9.668044n	9.567828	9.529775	9.937135

		A'	B'	C'	log sin a	log sin b	log sin c
Table VII.,	1863,	$118°\ 26'\ 43''.1$	$22°\ 43'\ 59''.7$	$47°\ 30'\ 1''.2$	9.992366	9.946935	9.700141
Table VIII.	$+30''.2$	+30.29	+30.41	+22.14	+0.9	−6.0	+15.9
	$- 3''.1$	+ 0.65	+ 2.26		+3.1	− 9.3
		118 27 13.4	22 44 30.8	47 30 25.6	9.992367	9.946932	9.700148

	M	t			
Table I., 1863	$155°\ 50'\ 9''.59$	+8.99932		cot $\frac{1}{2}M$	$90°\ 19'\ 42''.1$	7.758234n
April	20 38 10.95	0.24642	$\frac{1-e}{1+e}$ cot $\frac{1}{2}M =$ cot $\frac{1}{2}v'$	90 13 29.2	7.593650n
18 days	4 7 38.19	0.04928	v'	180 26 58.4	
5 hours	2 51.97	0.00057	From Table II. $c +$	29.3	
58 minutes	33.25		v	180 27 27.7	
15 seconds	0.14		cos v		9.999986n
	180 39 24.09	+9.29559	e cos v	−0.187243	9.272405n
			$1 + e$ cos v	+0.812757	9.909961

$M =$ mean anomaly, and $t =$ time since 1854.0.

r 0.496747

Formation of the Arguments from Table III.

	I.	II.	III.	IV.	V.	VI.	VII.	VIII.	IX.	X.
1863,	177.178	333.014	150.192	327.370	101.86	123.21	128.85	21.34	155.84	284.69
April,	352.523	13.158	5.680	358.200	46.94	18.83	33.79	331.89	20.64	54.43
18 days	358.504	2.632	1.136	359.640	9.39	3.76	6.76	354.38	4.12	10.89
6 hours	359.979	0.037	0.016	359.995	0.13	0.05	0.10	359.92	0.05	0.15
	168.184	348.841	157.024	325.205	158.32	145.85	169.50	347.53	180.65	350.16

	XI.	XII.	XIII.	XIV.	XV.	XVI.	XVII.	XVIII.	XIX.	XX.
1863,	144.55	96.22	225.51	80.5	198.5	74.9	15.7	117.6	321.7	273.4
April,	350.73	31.99	311.24	75.1	324.4	60.1	316.9	3.9	343.3	24.5
18 days	358.15	6.40	350.24	15.0	352.8	12.0	351.4	0.7	356.6	4.9
6 hours	359.98	0.09	359.86	0.2	359.9	0.2	359.9	0.0	359.9	0.1
	133.41	134.70	166.85	170.8	155.6	147.2	323.9	122.2	301.5	302.9

	XXI.	XXII.	XXIII.	XXIV.	XXV.	XXVI.	XXVII.	XXVIII.	XXIX.	XXX.
1863,	230.7	53.5	219.9	69.2	138.9	111.9	246.8	267.8	84.9	63.6
April,	80.7	88.2	206.3	45.2	335.8	348.9	283.2	9.6	2.1	30.2
18 days	16.2	17.6	347.2	9.0	355.2	357.8	344.7	2.0	0.4	6.1
6 hours	0.2	0.3	359.8	0.1	359.9	0.0	359.8	0.0	0.0	0.0
	327.8	159.6	143.2	123.5	109.8	98.6	154.5	279.4	87.4	90.9

	XXXI.	XXXII.	XXXIII.	XXXIV.	XXXV.	XXXVI.	XXXVII.	XXXVIII.	XXXIX.	XL.
1863,	236	133	48	316	182	42	10	70	5	219
April,	96	321	73	328	122	58	302	291	130	51
18 days	19	353	15	353	25	11	349	346	26	10
	351	87	136	277	329	111	301	347	161	280

	XLI.	XLII.	XLIII.	XLIV.	XLV.	XLVI.	XLVII.	XLVIII.	XLIX.
1863,	37	39	268	21	193	15	338	214	187
April,	43	116	255	87	310	71	143	281	294
18 days	9	23	330	18	350	14	29	345	347
	89	171	142	126	133	100	150	119	108

* The Arguments being expressed in degrees and decimals, 360.0, 720.0, or 1080.0, must be subtracted when one of the sums is greater than one of those numbers.

2

From Table IV.

	ξ' +	ξ' −	η' +	η' −	ζ' +	ζ' −			
ι	56.8		3460.1		134.8		$\cos(x_1 x)\ \xi'$	−	1558.3
I		5081.9	1559.0		368.8		$\cos(y_1 x)\ \eta'$	−	3380.7
II	4208.1		904.8			42.3	$\cos(z_1 x)\ \zeta'$	−	280.3
III	3079.5			596.9	236.2		ξ	−	5219.3
IV		3014.0	1418.0		227.6				
V		1403.9		271.7	1.4		$\cos(x_1 y)\ \xi'$	−	617.1
VI		677.8	849.5		706.6		$\cos(y_1 y)\ \eta'$	+	5894.0
VII	1009.3		151.2			83.9	$\cos(z_1 y)\ \zeta'$	−	702.1
VIII	101.6			25.2		63.1	η	+	4574.8
IX		216.9		23.0	113.4				
X		141.3		17.1	8.3		$\cos(x_1 z)\ \xi'$	−	666.8
XI		78.2	117.9		11.6		$\cos(y_1 z)\ \eta'$	+	2445.6
XII	81.1		39.7			48.3	$\cos(z_1 z)\ \zeta'$	+	1304.7
XIII		40.1	12.9		7.8		ζ	+	3083.5
XIV	40.8		6.4		0.9				
XV	718.5			130.8	20.6		$\sin(A'+v)$ 298 54 41.1		9.942191ₙ
XVI		366.4		125.6	6.8		$r \sin a$		0.480114
XVII		214.8		132.1	4.5		x		0.431305ₙ
XVIII	27.7			67.4	10.4		$\sin(B'+v)$ 203 11 58.5		9.595426ₙ
XIX	108.6			136.1	2.1		$r \sin b$		0.443679
XX		61.3	63.4			36.2	y		0.030104ₙ
XXI	94.6		34.3		1.0		$\sin(C'+v)$ 227 57 52.3		9.870833ₙ
XXII		91.3		19.8			$r \sin c$		0.196895
XXIII	44.7		20.3			0.5	z		0.067728ₙ
XXIV	31.6			54.3		5.5			
XXV		59.6		22.7			y	−	1.094218
XXVI		21.9		23.0			η	+	4575
XXVII	29.7			4.7			Y	+	0.438486
XXVIII	4.7			31.7			$\varDelta \cos \delta \sin a$	−	0.651157 9.813686ₙ
XXIX		10.2	5.0				x	−	2.609635
XXX	12.9			16.2		0.2	ξ	−	5219
XXXI		9.3		1.5			X	+	0.883932
XXXII	3.8			8.8			$\varDelta \cos \delta \cos a$	−	1.820922 0.260291ₙ
XXXIII	6.5			6.5		1.0	$\cos a$		9.973860ₙ
XXXIV	1.5			7.2			$\tan a$ 199 40 37.0		9.553395
XXXV	5.5			2.2					
XXXVI	8.5			5.8		1.8	z	−	1.168768
XXXVII	5.6			0.7			ζ	+	3084
XXXVIII	5.0			3.2		0.9	Z	+	0.190261
XXXIX		5.0		1.0			$\varDelta \sin \delta$	−	0.975423 9.989193ₙ
XL		0.5		2.1		1.2	$\varDelta \cos \delta$		0.286422
XLI		0.8		0.9			$\cos \delta$		9.950780
XLII	2.2			0.3			$\tan \delta$ −26 45 58.1		9.702771ₙ
XLIII	2.0			1.4					
XLIV	1.1			2.9			$\varDelta$		0.335642
XLV	1.1			1.8					
XLVI	2.2				1.1				
XLVII		1.1			0.5				
XLVIII		1.4			0.3				
XLIX		0.3			1.1				
	9694.2	11498.0	8811.3	1589.9	1827.9	319.9			
ξ', η', ζ'	−1803.8		+7221.5		+1507.9				

For the computation of an opposition ephemeris, only the secular perturbations and the first thirty terms will be necessary, since the remaining nineteen terms have no notable effect upon the geocentric place, the sum of them being always near zero. The ephemeris for 1863 from the manuscript Tables had been computed with those terms; from the above complete computation follows the correction of the ephemeris for April 18.5 in α —0^s.01 and in δ +$0''$.8. The comparison of a Berlin meridional observation on the 17th with the ephemeris gave comp. obs. in α +0^s.53 and in δ —$5''$.7, or, with the corrected ephemeris, +0^s.52 and $4.''9$. Since the perturbations by Saturn have been neglected, and this compared observation is four years after the last of the Normals used for the determination of the elements, the Tables can be considered satisfactory.

TABLE I.

FOR THE MEAN ANOMALY.

The times are referred to the meridian of Washington.

Years.	M	t	Years.	M	t
	° ′ ″			° ′ ″	
1851	230 50 40.20	− 3.00068	1876B	164 44 55.54	+22.00137
1852B	314 45 56.74	1.99863	1877	248 26 26.63	23.00068
1853	38 27 27.82	− 0.99932	1878	332 7 57.71	24.00000
1854	122 8 58.91	0.00000	1879	55 49 28.80	24.99932
1855	205 50 30.00	+ 0.99932	1880B	139 44 45.34	26.00137
1856B	289 45 46.54	2.00137	1881	223 26 16.43	27.00068
1857	13 27 17.62	3.00068	1882	307 7 47.51	28.00000
1858	97 8 48.71	4.00000	1883	30 49 18.60	28.99932
1859	180 50 19.80	4.99932	1884B	114 44 35.14	30.00137
1860B	264 45 36.34	6.00137	1885	198 26 6.23	31.00068
1861	348 27 7.42	7.00068	1886	282 7 37.31	32.00000
1862	72 8 38.51	8.00000	1887	5 49 8.40	32.99932
1863	155 50 9.59	8.99932	1888B	89 44 24.94	34.00137
1864B	239 45 26.14	10.00137	1889	173 25 56.03	35.00068
1865	323 26 57.22	11.00068	1890	257 7 27.11	36.00000
1866	47 8 28.32	12.00000	1891	340 48 58.20	36.99932
1867	130 49 59.40	12.99932	1892B	64 44 14.74	38.00137
1868B	214 45 15.94	14.00137	1893	148 25 45.82	39.00068
1869	298 26 47.03	15.00068	1894	232 7 16.91	40.00000
1870	22 8 18.12	16.00000	1895	315 48 48.00	40.99932
1871	105 49 49.20	16.99932	1896B	39 44 4.54	42.00137
1872B	189 45 5.74	18.00137	1897	123 25 35.62	43.00068
1873	273 26 36.83	19.00068	1898	207 7 6.71	44.00000
1874	357 8 7.92	20.00000	1899	290 48 37.80	44.99932
1875	80 49 39.00	+20.99932	1900B	14 43 54.34	+46.00137

Months.	M	t	Days.	M	t
	° ′ ″			° ′ ″	
January	0 0 0.00	+ 0.00000	1	0 13 45.46	+ 0.00274
February	7 6 29.11	0.08488	2	0 27 30.91	0.00548
March	13 31 41.85	0.16154	3	0 41 16.37	0.00821
April	20 38 10.95	0.24642	4	0 55 1.82	0.01095
May	27 30 54.60	0.32856	5	1 8 47.28	0.01369
June	34 37 23.71	0.41344	6	1 22 32.73	0.01643
July	41 30 7.36	0.49558	7	1 36 18.19	0.01917
August	48 36 36.47	0.58046	8	1 50 3.64	0.02190
September	55 43 5.57	0.66534	9	2 3 49.10	0.02464
October	62 35 49.22	0.74748	10	2 17 34.55	0.02738
November	69 42 18.33	0.83236	20	4 35 9.10	0.05476
December	76 35 1.98	+ 0.91450	30	6 52 43.65	+ 0.08214

In Bissextile Years one day must be subtracted from the date in the first two months.

TABLE I. — *Concluded.*

FOR THE MEAN ANOMALY.

The times are referred to the meridian of Washington.

Hours.	M	t	Hours.	M	t
1	0 34.39	+0.00011	13	7 27.12	+0.00149
2	1 8.79	0.00023	14	8 1.52	0.00160
3	1 43.18	0.00034	15	8 35.91	0.00172
4	2 17.58	0.00046	16	9 10.30	0.00183
5	2 51.97	0.00057	17	9 44.70	0.00195
6	3 26.36	0.00069	18	10 19.09	0.00206
7	4 0.76	0.00080	19	10 53.49	0.00218
8	4 35.15	0.00092	20	11 27.88	0.00229
9	5 9.55	0.00103	21	12 2.27	0.00241
10	5 43.94	0.00114	22	12 36.67	0.00252
11	6 18.33	0.00126	23	13 11.06	0.00264
12	6 52.73	+0.00137	24	13 45.46	+0.00275

	M			M	
	For Minutes.	For Seconds.		For Minutes.	For Seconds.
1	0.57	0.01	31	17.77	0.29
2	1.15	0.02	32	18.34	0.30
3	1.72	0.03	33	18.92	0.31
4	2.29	0.04	34	19.49	0.32
5	2.87	0.05	35	20.06	0.33
6	3.44	0.06	36	20.64	0.34
7	4.01	0.07	37	21.21	0.35
8	4.59	0.08	38	21.78	0.36
9	5.16	0.09	39	22.35	0.37
10	5.73	0.10	40	22.93	0.38
11	6.31	0.10	41	23.50	0.39
12	6.88	0.11	42	24.07	0.40
13	7.45	0.12	43	24.65	0.41
14	8.02	0.13	44	25.22	0.42
15	8.60	0.14	45	25.79	0.43
16	9.17	0.15	46	26.37	0.44
17	9.74	0.16	47	26.94	0.45
18	10.32	0.17	48	27.51	0.46
19	10.89	0.18	49	28.09	0.47
20	11.46	0.19	50	28.66	0.48
21	12.04	0.20	51	29.23	0.48
22	12.61	0.21	52	29.81	0.49
23	13.18	0.22	53	30.38	0.50
24	13.76	0.23	54	30.95	0.51
25	14.33	0.24	55	31.53	0.52
26	14.90	0.25	56	32.10	0.53
27	15.48	0.26	57	32.67	0.54
28	16.05	0.27	58	33.25	0.55
29	16.62	0.28	59	33.82	0.56
30	17.20	0.29	60	34.39	0.57

TABLE II.

FOR THE CORRECTION c TO BE ADDED TO THE AUXILIARY ANOMALY v'.

Argument = M. For $M > 180°$ the Argument is $360° - M$, and the sign of c to be reversed.

Arg.	c	Diff.	Arg.	c	Diff.	Arg.	c	Diff.	Arg.	c	Diff.
0.0	0 0.00	+47·32	22.5	+28 54.12	+22·08	45.0	+20 59.12	−17·97	67.5	+ 8 59.88	−33·35
.5	+ 0 47.32	47·28	23.0	29 16.20	21·14	.5	29 41.15	18·64	68.0	8 26.53	33·37
1.0	1 34.60	47·23	.5	29 37.34	20·18	46.0	29 22.51	19·30	.5	7 53.16	33·38
.5	2 21.83	47·16	24.0	29 57.52	19·22	.5	29 3.21	19·94	69.0	7 19.78	33·37
2.0	3 8.99	47·05	.5	30 16.74	18·26	47.0	28 43.27	20·57	.5	6 46.41	33·36
.5	3 56.04	46·90	25.0	30 35.00	17·29	.5	28 22.70	21·18	70.0	6 13.05	33·34
3.0	4 42.94	46·75	.5	30 52.29	16·33	48.0	28 1.52	21·78	.5	5 39.71	33·29
.5	5 29.68	46·55	26.0	31 8.62	15·37	.5	27 39.74	22·38	71.0	5 6.42	33·24
4.0	6 16.23	46·32	.5	31 23.99	14·39	49.0	27 17.39	22·92	.5	4 33.18	33·18
.5	7 2.55	46·07	27.0	31 38.38	13·43	.5	26 54.47	23·48	72.0	4 0.00	33·11
5.0	7 48.62	45·79	.5	31 51.81	12·45	50.0	26 30.99	24·01	.5	3 26.89	33·02
.5	8 34.41	45·46	28.0	32 4.26	11·48	.5	26 6.98	24·53	73.0	2 53.87	32·93
6.0	9 19.87	45·10	.5	32 15.74	10·50	51.0	25 42.45	25·04	.5	2 20.94	32·82
.5	10 4.97	44·74	29.0	32 26.24	9·53	.5	25 17.41	25·53	74.0	1 48.12	32·71
7.0	10 49.71	44·36	.5	32 35.77	8·55	52.0	24 51.88	26·01	.5	1 15.41	32·60
.5	11 34.07	43·95	30.0	32 44.32	7·58	.5	24 25.87	26·47	75.0	0 42.81	32·47
8.0	12 18.02	43·52	.5	32 51.90	6·62	53.0	23 59.40	26·91	.5	+ 0 10.34	32·31
.5	13 1.54	43·06	31.0	32 58.52	5·65	.5	23 32.49	27·34	76.0	− 0 21.97	32·17
9.0	13 44.60	42·58	.5	33 4.17	4·69	54.0	23 5.15	27·76	.5	0 54.14	32·01
.5	14 27.18	42·06	32.0	33 8.86	3·74	.5	22 37.39	28·15	77.0	1 26.15	31·84
10.0	15 9.24	41·54	.5	33 12.60	2·79	55.0	22 9.24	28·53	.5	1 57.99	31·67
.5	15 50.78	40·97	33.0	33 15.39	1·85	.5	21 40.71	28·89	78.0	2 29.66	31·48
11.0	16 31.75	40·39	.5	33 17.24	+0·91	56.0	21 11.82	29·23	.5	3 1.14	31·28
.5	17 12.14	39·77	34.0	33 18.15	−0·02	.5	20 42.59	29·58	79.0	3 32.42	31·08
12.0	17 51.91	39·12	.5	33 18.13	0·94	57.0	20 13.01	29·90	.5	4 3.50	30·87
.5	18 31.03	38·47	35.0	33 17.19	1·86	.5	19 43.11	30·21	80.0	4 34.37	30·66
13.0	19 9.50	37·80	.5	33 15.33	2·76	58.0	19 12.90	30·50	.5	5 5.03	30·43
.5	19 47.30	37·12	36.0	33 12.57	3·66	.5	18 42.40	30·78	81.0	5 35.46	30·20
14.0	20 24.42	36·43	.5	33 8.91	4·55	59.0	18 11.62	31·05	.5	6 5.66	29·96
.5	21 0.85	35·70	37.0	33 4.36	5·44	.5	17 40.57	31·31	82.0	6 35.62	29·72
15.0	21 36.55	34·96	.5	32 58.92	6·31	60.0	17 9.26	31·52	.5	7 5.34	29·46
.5	22 11.51	34·20	38.0	32 52.61	7·18	.5	16 37.74	31·73	83.0	7 34.80	29·20
16.0	22 45.71	33·43	.5	32 45.43	8·02	61.0	16 6.01	31·94	.5	8 4.00	28·93
.5	23 19.14	32·63	39.0	32 37.41	8·86	.5	15 34.07	32·13	84.0	8 32.93	28·66
17.0	23 51.77	31·82	.5	32 28.55	9·69	62.0	15 1.94	32·31	.5	9 1.59	28·38
.5	24 23.59	30·98	40.0	32 18.86	10·51	.5	14 29.63	32·47	85.0	9 29.97	28·10
18.0	24 54.57	30·12	.5	32 8.35	11·31	63.0	13 57.16	32·62	.5	9 58.07	27·81
.5	25 24.69	29·27	41.0	31 57.04	12·10	.5	13 24.54	32·75	86.0	10 25.88	27·52
19.0	25 53.96	28·41	.5	31 44.94	12·88	64.0	12 51.79	32·88	.5	10 53.40	27·21
.5	26 22.37	27·54	42.0	31 32.06	13·65	.5	12 18.91	32·98	87.0	11 20.61	26·91
20.0	26 49.91	26·65	.5	31 18.41	14·40	65.0	11 45.93	33·08	.5	11 47.52	26·60
.5	27 16.56	25·76	43.0	31 4.01	15·14	.5	11 12.85	33·15	88.0	12 14.12	26·28
21.0	27 42.32	24·85	.5	30 48.87	15·87	66.0	10 39.70	33·22	.5	12 40.40	25·96
.5	28 7.17	23·94	44.0	30 33.00	16·59	.5	10 6.48	33·28	89.0	13 6.36	25·64
22.0	28 31.11	+23·01	.5	30 16.41	−17·29	67.0	9 33.20	−33·32	.5	13 32.00	−25·30
.5	+28 54.12		45.0	+29 59.12		.5	+ 8 59.88		90.0	−13 57.30	

$$\cot \tfrac{1}{2} v' = \frac{1-e}{1+e} \cot \tfrac{1}{2} M$$

$$r = \frac{p}{1 + e \cos v}$$

True Anomaly $v = v' + c$

$\log p = 0.4067081$

$\log \dfrac{1-e}{1+e} = 9.8354158$

$\log e = 9.2724191$

TABLE II.— *Concluded.*

FOR THE CORRECTION c TO BE ADDED TO THE AUXILIARY ANOMALY v'.

Argument = M. For $M > 180°$ the Argument is $360° - M$, and the sign of c to be reversed.

Arg.	c	Diff.	Arg.	c	Diff.	Arg.	c	Diff.	Arg.	c	Diff.
°	′ ″	″	°	′ ″	″	°	′ ″	″	°	′ ″	″
90.0	−13 57.30	24.98	112.5	−26 30.64	7.73	135.0	−26 10.44	8.27	157.5	−15 44.57	18.68
.5	14 22.28	24.64	113.0	26 38.37	7.33	.5	26 2.17	8.57	158.0	15 25.89	18.84
91.0	14 46.92	24.29	.5	26 45.70	6.98	136.0	25 53.60	8.87	.5	15 7.05	18.98
.5	15 11.21	23.94	114.0	26 52.63	6.54	.5	25 44.73	9.16	159.0	14 48.07	19.14
92.0	15 35.15	23.60	.5	26 59.17	6.15	137.0	25 35.57	9.46	.5	14 28.93	19.28
.5	15 58.75	23.24	115.0	27 5.32	5.76	.5	25 26.11	9.74	160.0	14 9.65	19.40
93.0	16 21.99	22.89	.5	27 11.08	5.37	138.0	25 16.37	10.03	.5	13 50.25	19.54
.5	16 44.88	22.53	116.0	27 16.45	4.98	.5	25 6.34	10.32	161.0	13 30.70	19.69
94.0	17 7.41	22.17	.5	27 21.43	4.60	139.0	24 56.02	10.59	.5	13 11.01	19.82
.5	17 29.58	21.80	117.0	27 26.03	4.22	.5	24 45.43	10.87	162.0	12 51.19	19.95
95.0	17 51.38	21.43	.5	27 30.25	3.93	140.0	24 34.56	11.15	.5	12 31.24	20.08
.5	18 12.81	21.06	118.0	27 34.18	3.35	.5	24 23.41	11.41	163.0	12 11.16	20.19
96.0	18 33.87	20.69	.5	27 37.53	3.08	141.0	24 12.00	11.68	.5	11 50.97	20.32
.5	18 54.55	20.32	119.0	27 40.61	2.69	.5	24 0.32	11.95	164.0	11 30.65	20.42
97.0	19 14.87	19.93	.5	27 43.30	2.32	142.0	23 48.37	12.20	.5	11 10.23	20.54
.5	19 34.80	19.55	120.0	27 45.62	1.96	.5	23 36.17	12.47	165.0	10 49.69	20.64
98.0	19 54.35	19.17	.5	27 47.57	1.57	143.0	23 23.70	12.72	.5	10 29.05	20.75
.5	20 13.52	18.79	121.0	27 49.14	1.20	.5	23 10.98	12.97	166.0	10 8.30	20.84
99.0	20 32.31	18.41	.5	27 50.34	0.83	144.0	22 58.01	13.22	.5	9 47.46	20.94
.5	20 50.72	18.01	122.0	27 51.17	0.47	.5	22 44.79	13.46	167.0	9 26.52	21.03
100.0	21 8.73	17.63	.5	27 51.61	− 0.10	145.0	22 31.33	13.71	.5	9 5.49	21.12
.5	21 26.36	17.24	123.0	27 51.74	+ 0.26	.5	22 17.62	13.95	168.0	8 44.37	21.21
101.0	21 43.60	16.85	.5	27 51.48	0.63	146.0	22 3.67	14.18	.5	8 23.16	21.29
.5	22 0.45	16.45	124.0	27 50.85	0.99	.5	21 49.49	14.41	169.0	8 1.87	21.37
102.0	22 16.90	16.06	.5	27 49.86	1.34	147.0	21 35.08	14.65	.5	7 40.50	21.44
.5	22 32.96	15.66	125.0	27 48.52	1.69	.5	21 20.43	14.87	170.0	7 19.06	21.51
103.0	22 48.62	15.27	.5	27 46.83	1.89	148.0	21 5.56	15.09	.5	6 57.55	21.58
.5	23 3.89	14.87	126.0	27 44.78	2.39	.5	20 50.47	15.31	171.0	6 35.97	21.64
104.0	23 18.76	14.48	.5	27 42.39	2.75	149.0	20 35.16	15.53	.5	6 14.33	21.71
.5	23 33.24	14.07	127.0	27 39.64	3.09	.5	20 19.63	15.73	172.0	5 52.62	21.77
105.0	23 47.31	13.68	.5	27 36.55	3.44	150.0	20 3.90	15.95	.5	5 30.85	21.81
.5	24 0.99	13.28	128.0	27 33.11	3.77	.5	19 47.95	16.15	173.0	5 9.04	21.86
106.0	24 14.27	12.88	.5	27 29.34	4.12	151.0	19 31.80	16.36	.5	4 47.18	21.91
.5	24 27.15	12.49	129.0	27 25.22	4.44	.5	19 15.44	16.56	174.0	4 25.27	21.96
107.0	24 39.64	12.09	.5	27 20.78	4.79	152.0	18 58.88	16.75	.5	4 3.31	21.99
.5	24 51.73	11.68	130.0	27 15.99	5.11	.5	18 42.13	16.94	175.0	3 41.32	22.04
108.0	25 3.41	11.27	.5	27 10.88	5.44	153.0	18 25.19	17.13	.5	3 19.28	22.06
.5	25 14.68	10.88	131.0	27 5.44	5.76	.5	18 8.06	17.32	176.0	2 57.22	22.09
109.0	25 25.56	10.49	.5	26 59.63	6.09	154.0	17 50.74	17.51	.5	2 35.13	22.09
.5	25 36.05	10.08	132.0	26 53.59	6.40	.5	17 33.23	17.69	177.0	2 13.01	22.14
110.0	25 46.13	9.70	.5	26 47.19	6.73	155.0	17 15.55	17.85	.5	1 50.87	22.13
.5	25 55.83	9.29	133.0	26 40.46	7.04	.5	16 57.70	18.02	178.0	1 28.72	22.15
111.0	26 5.12	8.90	.5	26 33.42	7.35	156.0	16 39.68	18.20	.5	1 6.55	22.17
.5	26 14.02	8.51	134.0	26 26.07	7.66	.5	16 21.48	18.38	179.0	0 44.37	22.18
112.0	26 22.53	8.11	.5	26 18.41	7.97	157.0	16 3.10	18.53	.5	− 0 22.18	22.19
.5	−26 30.64		135.0	−26 10.44		.5	−15 44.57		180.0	0 0.00	+22.18

$$\cot \tfrac{1}{2} v' = \frac{1-e}{1+e} \cot \tfrac{1}{2} M$$

True Anomaly $v = v' + c$

$$\log \frac{1-e}{1+e} = 9.8354158$$

$$r = \frac{p}{1 + e \cos v}$$

$\log p = 0.4067081$

$\log e = 9.2724191$

TABLE III.
FOR THE ARGUMENTS.

A. For the different Years. The times are referred to the meridian of Washington.

Years.	I.	II.	III.	IV.	V.	VI.	VII.	VIII.	IX.	X.
	°	°	°	°	°	°	°	°	°	°
1851	181.332	52.177	233.509	54.841	335.20	285.69	283.02	310.49	230.84	153.87
1852*B*	150.924	105.668	256.613	47.536	166.14	2.30	60.45	196.16	314.77	15.22
1853	120.598	159.056	279.654	40.252	356.57	78.71	197.51	82.14	38.46	235.07
1854	90.273	212.422	302.695	32.968	186.99	155.12	334.57	328.12	122.15	96.72
1855	59.947	265.789	325.736	25.683	17.41	231.52	111.63	214.11	205.84	317.47
1856*B*	29.539	319.301	348.840	18.378	208.37	308.14	249.06	99.78	289.76	178.83
1857	359.213	12.668	11.881	11.094	38.79	24.55	26.12	345.76	13.45	39.58
1858	328.888	66.035	34.922	3.810	220.22	100.96	163.18	231.74	97.15	260.33
1859	298.562	119.401	57.964	356.526	50.64	177.36	300.24	117.72	180.84	121.08
1860*B*	268.154	192.014	81.068	349.222	230.50	253.98	77.67	3.39	264.76	342.43
1861	237.828	226.221	104.109	341.937	81.01	330.39	214.73	249.38	348.45	203.18
1862	207.503	279.647	127.150	334.653	271.44	46.80	351.79	135.36	72.14	63.94
1863	177.178	333.014	150.192	327.370	101.86	123.21	128.85	21.34	155.84	284.69
1864*B*	146.769	26.527	173.206	320.065	292.81	199.82	266.28	267.01	230.76	146.04
1865	116.444	79.893	196.337	312.781	123.23	276.23	43.34	152.99	323.45	6.79
1866	86.119	133.260	219.379	305.497	313.66	352.64	180.40	38.98	47.14	227.54
1867	55.793	186.627	242.420	298.213	144.09	69.05	317.46	284.96	130.83	89.29
1868*B*	25.385	240.139	265.524	290.009	335.03	145.66	94.89	170.63	214.73	309.65
1869	355.060	293.506	288.566	283.626	165.46	222.07	231.95	56.61	298.45	170.40
1870	324.734	346.873	311.607	276.342	355.88	298.48	9.01	302.60	22.14	31.15
1871	294.409	40.240	334.649	269.058	186.31	14.89	146.07	188.58	105.83	251.90
1872*B*	264.001	93.753	357.753	261.754	17.26	91.51	283.50	74.25	189.75	113.26
1873	233.676	147.119	20.795	254.471	207.69	167.91	60.56	320.23	273.44	334.01
1874	203.350	200.486	43.836	247.187	38.11	244.32	197.62	206.21	357.14	194.76
1875	173.025	253.853	66.878	239.904	228.53	320.73	334.68	92.20	80.83	55.51
1876*B*	142.617	307.366	89.983	232.600	59.48	37.35	112.11	337.87	164.75	276.86
1877	112.292	0.733	113.025	225.316	240.91	113.76	249.17	223.85	248.44	137.61
1878	81.967	54.100	136.067	218.033	80.33	190.17	26.23	109.83	332.13	358.36
1879	51.642	107.467	159.108	210.750	270.76	266.57	163.29	355.82	55.82	219.12
1880*B*	21.234	160.080	182.213	203.447	101.70	343.19	300.73	241.49	139.75	80.47
1881	350.908	214.046	205.255	196.163	292.13	59.60	77.78	127.47	223.44	301.22
1882	320.583	267.713	228.296	188.879	122.55	136.01	214.84	13.45	307.13	161.97
1883	290.258	321.080	251.337	181.595	312.98	212.42	351.90	259.44	30.82	22.72
1884*B*	259.849	14.592	274.441	174.290	143.93	289.03	129.34	145.11	114.74	244.08
1885	229.524	67.959	297.483	167.007	334.35	5.44	266.39	31.09	198.44	104.83
1886	199.198	121.326	320.524	159.723	164.78	81.85	43.45	277.07	282.13	325.58
1887	168.873	174.692	343.566	152.439	355.20	158.26	180.51	163.05	5.92	186.33
1888*B*	138.465	228.205	6.670	145.134	186.15	234.87	317.94	48.72	89.74	47.69
1889	108.139	281.572	29.711	137.851	16.58	311.28	95.00	294.71	173.43	268.44
1890	77.814	334.939	52.753	130.567	207.00	27.69	232.06	180.60	257.12	129.19
1891	47.489	28.305	75.794	123.283	37.43	104.10	9.12	66.67	340.82	340.94
1892*B*	17.080	81.818	98.898	115.978	228.37	180.72	146.56	312.34	64.74	211.29
1893	346.755	135.185	121.940	108.695	58.80	257.12	283.61	198.33	148.43	72.04
1894	316.430	188.551	144.981	101.410	249.22	333.53	60.67	84.31	232.12	292.79
1895	286.104	241.918	168.022	94.127	79.65	49.94	197.73	330.29	315.81	153.55
1896*B*	255.696	295.430	191.126	86.822	270.60	126.56	335.16	215.96	39.73	14.00
1897	225.371	348.797	214.168	79.538	101.02	202.96	112.22	101.04	123.43	235.65
1898	195.045	42.164	237.209	72.254	291.45	279.37	249.28	347.93	207.12	96.40
1899	164.720	95.530	260.250	64.970	121.87	355.78	26.34	233.01	290.81	317.15
1900*B*	134.311	149.043	283.355	57.666	312.82	72.40	163.78	119.58	14.73	178.51

TABLE III. — *Continued.*
FOR THE ARGUMENTS.
A. For the different Years. The times are referred to the meridian of Washington.

Years.	XI.	XII.	XIII.	XIV.	XV.	XVI.	XVII.	XVIII.	XIX.	XX.
1851	236.17	337.86	70.64	24.7	131.8	27.4	313.2	288.3	57.5	159.2
1852*B*	198.46	107.99	241.39	330.0	347.1	271.8	138.0	304.1	340.4	258.9
1853	160.85	237.77	43.68	274.4	202.7	155.6	323.3	319.9	281.4	358.4
1854	123.24	7.54	205.97	218.9	58.4	39.4	148.7	335.7	213.5	97.8
1855	85.63	137.31	8.26	163.3	274.1	283.2	334.0	351.4	145.6	197.3
1856*B*	47.92	267.44	170.01	108.6	129.3	167.7	158.9	7.2	77.5	297.0
1857	10.31	37.22	332.30	53.0	345.0	51.5	344.2	23.0	9.5	36.4
1858	332.70	166.99	134.59	357.5	200.6	295.2	169.5	38.7	301.6	135.9
1859	295.09	296.77	296.88	301.9	56.3	179.0	354.8	54.5	233.6	235.3
1860*B*	257.38	66.90	98.63	247.2	271.5	63.5	179.7	70.3	165.5	335.0
1861	219.77	196.67	260.92	191.6	127.2	307.3	5.0	86.0	97.6	74.5
1862	182.15	326.44	63.21	136.1	342.9	191.1	190.4	101.8	29.7	173.9
1863	144.55	96.22	225.51	80.5	198.5	74.9	15.7	117.6	321.7	273.4
1864*B*	106.83	296.35	27.26	25.8	53.8	319.3	200.6	133.4	253.6	13.1
1865	69.22	356.12	189.55	330.2	269.4	203.1	25.9	149.1	165.7	112.6
1866	31.62	125.90	351.84	274.7	125.1	86.9	211.2	164.9	117.7	212.0
1867	354.01	255.67	154.13	219.1	340.8	330.7	36.5	180.6	49.8	311.5
1868*B*	316.29	25.80	315.86	164.4	196.0	215.2	221.4	196.4	341.7	51.2
1869	278.68	155.58	118.17	108.8	51.7	99.0	46.7	212.2	273.7	151.6
1870	241.08	285.35	280.46	53.3	267.3	342.8	232.1	227.9	205.8	250.1
1871	203.47	55.13	82.75	357.7	123.0	226.5	57.4	243.7	137.9	349.5
1872*B*	165.75	185.26	244.50	303.0	338.2	111.0	242.3	259.5	69.8	89.3
1873	128.15	315.03	46.79	247.4	193.9	354.8	67.6	275.3	1.8	188.7
1874	90.54	84.81	209.08	191.9	49.6	236.6	252.9	291.0	293.9	288.2
1875	52.93	214.58	11.37	136.3	265.2	122.4	78.2	306.8	226.0	27.6
1876*B*	15.22	344.71	173.12	81.6	120.5	6.8	263.1	322.6	157.8	127.3
1877	337.61	114.49	335.41	26.1	336.1	250.6	86.4	338.3	89.9	226.8
1878	300.00	244.27	137.70	330.5	191.8	134.4	273.8	354.1	22.0	326.2
1879	262.39	14.04	299.99	274.9	47.5	18.2	99.1	9.9	314.0	65.7
1880*B*	224.68	144.17	101.74	220.2	262.7	262.7	284.0	25.7	245.9	165.4
1881	187.07	273.95	264.03	164.7	118.4	146.5	109.3	41.4	178.0	264.9
1882	149.46	43.72	66.32	109.1	334.0	30.3	294.6	57.2	110.0	4.3
1883	111.85	173.50	228.61	53.5	189.7	274.1	120.0	72.9	42.1	103.7
1884*B*	74.14	303.63	30.36	358.8	45.0	158.5	304.8	88.7	334.0	203.5
1885	36.53	73.40	192.65	303.3	260.6	42.3	130.1	104.5	266.1	302.9
1886	358.92	203.18	354.94	247.7	116.3	286.1	315.5	120.2	198.1	42.4
1887	321.31	332.95	157.23	192.2	331.9	169.9	140.8	136.0	130.2	141.8
1888*B*	283.60	103.08	318.08	137.6	187.2	54.4	325.7	151.8	62.1	241.5
1889	245.99	232.85	121.27	81.9	42.8	298.1	151.0	167.6	354.1	341.0
1890	208.38	2.63	283.57	26.3	258.6	181.9	336.3	183.3	286.2	80.4
1891	170.77	132.40	85.86	330.7	114.2	65.7	161.6	199.1	218.3	179.9
1892*B*	133.06	262.53	247.60	276.0	329.4	310.2	346.5	214.9	150.1	279.6
1893	95.45	32.31	49.90	220.5	185.1	194.0	171.8	230.6	82.2	19.1
1894	57.84	162.08	212.19	164.9	40.7	77.8	357.2	246.4	14.3	118.5
1895	20.23	291.86	14.46	109.4	256.4	321.6	182.5	262.1	206.3	218.0
1896*B*	342.52	61.99	176.23	54.6	111.7	206.0	7.4	277.9	238.2	317.7
1897	304.91	191.76	338.52	359.1	327.3	89.8	192.7	293.7	170.3	57.1
1898	267.30	321.54	140.81	303.5	182.9	333.6	18.0	309.5	102.3	156.6
1899	229.69	91.31	303.10	248.0	38.6	217.4	203.3	325.2	34.4	256.0
1900*B*	191.98	222.44	104.85	193.2	253.9	101.9	18.2	341.0	326.3	355.7

TABLE III.— *Continued.*

FOR THE ARGUMENTS.

A. For the different Years. The times are referred to the meridian of Washington.

Years.	XXI.	XXII.	XXIII.	XXIV.	XXV.	XXVI.	XXVII.	XXVIII.	XXIX.	XXX.
	°	°	°	°	°	°	°	°	°	°
1851	238.2	76.9	82.2	30.0	238.8	291.0	30.1	161.9	343.2	32.7
1852 *B*	236.6	75.7	183.2	213.7	140.3	246.0	77.5	200.8	351.7	155.5
1853	194.1	73.5	284.9	36.8	42.0	201.1	125.8	239.6	0.2	278.0
1854	161.6	71.3	26.5	220.0	303.8	156.2	174.1	278.4	8.6	40.5
1855	129.0	69.1	128.2	43.1	205.5	111.3	229.4	317.2	17.1	163.0
1856 *B*	97.4	67.0	229.1	226.7	107.0	66.3	269.8	356.1	25.6	285.8
1857	64.9	65.7	330.7	49.9	8.7	21.4	318.1	34.9	34.1	48.3
1858	32.4	63.5	72.4	233.0	270.5	336.5	6.3	73.7	42.5	170.8
1859	359.9	61.3	174.0	56.2	172.2	291.6	54.6	112.5	51.0	293.3
1860 *B*	328.3	60.1	274.9	239.8	73.7	246.6	102.0	151.4	59.5	56.1
1861	295.7	57.9	16.6	63.0	335.4	201.7	150.3	190.2	68.0	178.6
1862	263.2	55.7	118.2	246.1	237.2	156.8	198.6	229.0	76.5	301.1
1863	230.7	53.5	219.9	69.2	138.9	111.9	246.8	267.8	84.9	63.6
1864 *B*	199.1	55.3	320.8	252.0	40.4	66.9	294.3	306.7	93.4	186.4
1865	166.6	50.1	62.4	76.0	362.1	22.0	342.5	345.5	101.9	308.9
1866	134.1	47.9	161.1	259.1	203.9	337.1	30.8	24.3	110.4	71.4
1867	101.5	45.8	265.7	82.3	105.6	292.2	79.1	63.1	118.8	193.9
1868 *B*	69.9	44.5	6.6	265.9	7.1	247.2	126.5	102.0	127.3	316.7
1869	37.4	42.4	108.3	89.1	268.8	202.3	174.8	140.8	135.8	79.2
1870	4.9	40.1	209.9	272.2	170.5	157.4	223.1	179.6	144.3	201.7
1871	332.4	38.0	311.6	95.4	72.3	112.5	271.3	218.4	152.8	324.2
1872 *B*	300.8	36.8	52.5	279.0	333.8	67.6	318.7	257.3	161.3	87.0
1873	268.2	34.6	154.1	102.2	235.5	22.6	7.0	296.1	169.7	209.5
1874	235.7	32.4	255.8	285.3	137.2	337.7	55.3	334.9	178.2	332.0
1875	203.2	30.2	357.4	108.4	39.0	292.8	103.6	13.7	186.7	94.5
1876 *B*	171.6	29.0	98.4	292.1	300.5	247.8	151.0	52.6	195.2	217.3
1877	139.1	26.8	200.0	115.2	202.2	202.9	199.3	91.4	203.7	339.8
1878	106.6	24.6	301.6	298.4	103.9	158.0	247.6	130.2	212.1	102.3
1879	74.0	22.4	43.3	121.5	5.7	113.1	255.8	169.0	220.6	224.8
1880 *B*	42.4	21.2	144.2	305.2	267.1	68.1	343.2	207.9	229.1	347.6
1881	9.9	19.0	245.8	128.3	168.9	23.2	31.5	246.7	237.6	110.1
1882	337.9	16.8	347.5	311.4	70.6	338.3	79.8	285.5	246.1	232.6
1883	304.9	14.6	89.1	134.6	332.4	293.4	128.0	324.3	254.5	355.1
1884 *B*	273.3	13.4	190.1	318.2	233.8	248.4	175.5	3.2	263.0	117.9
1885	240.7	11.2	291.7	141.4	135.6	203.5	223.7	42.0	271.5	240.4
1886	208.2	9.0	33.3	324.5	37.3	158.6	272.0	80.8	280.0	2.9
1887	175.7	6.8	135.0	147.6	299.1	113.7	320.3	119.6	288.4	125.4
1888 *B*	144.1	5.6	235.0	331.3	200.5	68.7	7.7	158.5	296.9	248.2
1889	111.6	3.4	337.6	154.4	102.3	23.8	56.0	197.3	305.4	10.7
1890	79.1	1.3	79.2	337.6	4.0	338.9	104.3	236.1	313.9	133.2
1891	46.5	359.0	180.8	160.7	265.7	294.0	152.5	274.9	322.4	255.7
1892 *B*	14.9	357.8	281.8	344.4	167.2	249.0	199.9	313.8	330.9	18.5
1893	342.4	355.7	23.4	167.5	69.0	204.1	248.2	352.6	339.3	141.0
1894	309.9	353.5	125.0	350.6	330.7	159.2	296.5	31.4	347.9	263.5
1895	277.4	351.3	226.7	173.8	232.4	114.3	344.8	70.2	356.3	26.0
1896 *B*	245.8	350.1	327.6	357.4	133.9	69.3	32.2	109.1	4.8	148.8
1897	213.2	347.9	69.3	180.6	35.6	24.4	80.5	147.9	13.2	271.3
1898	180.7	345.7	170.9	3.7	297.4	339.5	128.7	186.7	21.7	33.8
1899	148.2	343.5	272.5	186.8	199.1	294.6	177.0	225.5	30.2	156.3
1900 *B*	116.6	342.5	13.5	10.5	100.6	249.6	224.4	264.4	38.7	279.1

19

TABLE III. — *Continued.*

FOR THE ARGUMENTS.

A. For the different Years. The times are referred to the meridian of Washington.

Years.	XXXI.	XXXII.	XXXIII.	XXXIV.	XXXV.	XXXVI.	XXXVII.	XXXVIII	XXXIX.	XL.
	°	°	°	°	°	°	°	°	°	°
1851	256	242	60	60	0	62	316	209	179	264
1852B	285	82	18	201	136	319	80	287	345	110
1853	313	283	315	163	271	196	205	5	150	316
1854	341	124	252	34	46	72	329	84	316	163
1855	9	325	189	266	161	300	94	162	121	9
1856B	38	166	127	137	317	186	218	240	287	216
1857	67	7	64	8	92	63	343	319	93	62
1858	95	208	1	239	227	299	107	37	258	268
1859	123	49	299	111	2	176	232	116	63	114
1860B	152	250	236	342	138	53	356	194	230	321
1861	180	91	174	213	273	249	121	273	35	107
1862	208	292	111	85	48	166	245	351	200	13
1863	236	133	48	316	182	42	10	70	5	219
1864B	266	334	346	187	319	270	134	148	172	66
1865	294	175	283	59	94	156	259	226	337	272
1866	322	16	220	290	228	32	24	305	142	119
1867	350	217	157	161	3	269	148	23	307	325
1868B	19	58	95	32	139	146	272	101	114	171
1869	47	259	33	264	274	23	37	180	279	18
1870	75	100	330	135	49	250	162	258	84	224
1871	104	301	267	7	184	136	296	337	250	70
1872B	133	142	205	238	320	13	50	55	56	277
1873	161	343	142	109	95	249	175	133	229	123
1874	189	184	79	341	230	126	300	212	27	329
1875	217	25	16	212	6	2	64	291	192	175
1876B	246	226	314	63	141	239	188	8	359	22
1877	275	67	251	315	276	116	313	87	164	228
1878	303	268	189	186	51	353	78	166	329	74
1879	331	109	126	57	186	229	202	244	134	281
1880B	0	310	64	288	322	106	326	322	301	127
1881	28	141	1	160	97	343	91	41	106	334
1882	56	352	298	31	232	219	216	119	271	180
1883	84	193	235	263	7	96	341	198	76	26
1884B	114	34	173	134	143	333	105	276	243	233
1885	142	235	110	5	278	209	229	354	48	79
1886	170	176	47	237	53	86	354	73	213	285
1887	198	277	345	108	187	322	119	151	19	131
1888B	227	118	283	339	324	200	243	229	185	338
1889	255	319	220	210	98	76	7	308	350	184
1890	283	160	157	82	233	313	132	26	156	30
1891	312	1	94	313	8	189	257	105	321	237
1892B	341	201	32	184	144	66	21	183	127	63
1893	9	43	329	66	270	303	145	262	293	289
1894	37	244	266	287	54	170	270	340	98	136
1895	65	85	204	159	189	56	35	59	263	342
1896B	94	235	142	30	325	293	160	137	70	189
1897	123	126	79	261	100	169	283	215	235	85
1898	151	328	16	132	235	46	48	293	40	241
1899	179	169	313	4	10	282	173	12	205	87
1900B	208	9	251	235	146	160	297	90	12	294

TABLE III.— *Continued.*
FOR THE ARGUMENTS.

A. For the different Years.   The times are referred to the meridian of Washington.

Years.	XLI.	XLII.	XLIII.	XLIV.	XLV.	XLVI.	XLVII.	XLVIII.	XLIX.
1851	85	126	341	132	134	134	231	85	137
1852B	261	240	274	123	289	65	91	125	231
1853	77	351	208	114	84	355	309	166	325
1854	253	103	142	104	239	285	168	207	59
1855	60	215	76	95	34	215	27	248	154
1856B	245	328	10	86	188	145	247	288	247
1857	61	80	304	77	343	75	105	329	342
1858	237	192	236	67	138	5	324	10	76
1859	53	304	172	58	293	295	181	51	171
1860B	229	57	105	49	88	226	43	91	264
1861	45	169	40	40	243	155	261	132	359
1862	221	280	334	30	38	85	120	173	93
1863	37	32	268	21	193	15	338	214	187
1864B	213	145	201	12	347	306	198	254	281
1865	29	257	136	3	142	236	57	295	15
1866	205	9	70	353	297	166	275	336	110
1867	21	121	4	344	92	96	134	17	204
1868B	197	234	297	335	247	26	354	57	298
1869	13	346	231	326	42	316	213	98	32
1870	189	98	166	317	197	246	71	139	126
1871	4	209	100	307	352	176	290	180	221
1872B	191	323	33	299	146	107	150	221	314
1873	357	74	327	289	301	36	9	261	49
1874	172	186	262	280	96	326	227	302	143
1875	348	298	196	270	251	256	86	343	237
1876B	165	51	129	262	46	187	306	24	331
1877	341	163	63	252	201	117	164	65	65
1878	156	275	357	243	356	47	23	106	160
1879	332	27	292	233	151	336	242	147	254
1880B	149	140	225	225	305	267	102	187	348
1881	324	252	159	215	100	197	320	228	82
1882	140	3	93	206	255	127	179	269	176
1883	316	115	27	196	50	57	37	310	271
1884B	133	228	321	188	205	347	257	350	4
1885	308	340	233	178	0	277	116	31	99
1886	124	92	189	169	155	207	335	72	193
1887	300	204	123	159	310	137	193	113	288
1888B	116	317	56	151	104	68	53	153	21
1889	292	69	351	141	250	358	272	194	115
1890	108	181	235	132	54	287	130	235	210
1891	284	292	219	122	200	217	349	276	304
1892B	100	46	152	114	4	147	209	316	38
1893	276	157	87	104	159	78	68	357	132
1894	92	269	21	95	314	8	286	38	226
1895	268	21	315	85	109	298	145	79	321
1896B	86	134	246	77	263	298	5	119	54
1897	260	246	182	67	58	158	224	160	149
1898	76	358	117	58	213	88	82	201	243
1899	252	110	51	48	8	18	301	242	338
1900B	68	223	344	40	163	308	161	284	71

TABLE III. — *Continued.*

FOR THE ARGUMENTS.

B. Variations of the Arguments for the different Months. The times are referred to the meridian of Washington.

Months.	I.	II.	III.	IV.	V.	VI.	VII.	VIII.	IX.	X.
	o	o	o	o	o	o	o	o	o	o
January	0.000	0.000	0.000	0.000	0.00	0.00	0.00	0.00	0.00	0.00
February	357.425	4.532	1.956	359.380	16.17	6.49	11.64	350.32	7.11	18.75
March	355.098	8.626	3.724	358.820	30.77	12.34	22.15	341.57	13.53	35.60
April	352.523	13.159	5.680	358.200	46.94	18.83	33.79	331.89	20.64	54.43
May	350.031	17.544	7.573	357.600	62.59	25.11	45.06	322.51	27.51	72.58
June	347.456	22.076	9.530	356.980	78.76	31.60	56.70	312.83	34.62	91.33
July	344.964	26.462	11.423	356.380	94.41	37.88	67.96	303.46	41.50	109.47
August	342.380	30.994	13.379	355.760	110.58	44.37	79.60	293.77	48.61	128.22
September	339.814	35.526	15.336	355.140	126.75	50.86	91.24	284.09	55.72	146.97
October	337.322	39.912	17.229	354.540	142.40	57.14	102.51	274.72	62.60	165.11
November	334.747	44.444	19.185	353.920	158.57	63.63	114.15	265.03	69.71	183.86
December	332.255	48.830	21.079	353.320	174.22	69.91	125.41	255.66	76.58	202.01

Months.	XI.	XII.	XIII.	XIV.	XV.	XVI.	XVII.	XVIII.	XIX.	XX.
	o	o	o	o	o	o	o	o	o	o
January	0.00	0.00	0.00	0.0	0.0	0.0	0.0	0.0	0.0	0.0
February	356.80	11.02	343.21	25.9	347.7	20.7	345.2	1.3	354.2	8.4
March	353.92	20.97	328.03	49.2	336.7	39.4	331.8	2.5	349.0	16.1
April	350.73	31.99	311.24	75.1	324.4	60.1	316.9	3.9	343.3	24.5
May	347.63	42.66	294.99	100.1	312.5	80.2	302.6	5.2	337.7	32.7
June	344.44	53.63	278.20	125.9	300.3	100.9	287.7	6.5	331.9	41.1
July	341.34	64.31	261.95	150.9	288.4	120.9	273.4	7.8	326.3	49.3
August	338.15	75.36	245.15	176.8	276.1	141.6	258.5	9.1	320.6	57.7
September	334.95	86.38	228.36	202.6	263.9	162.3	243.7	10.4	314.8	66.2
October	331.86	97.05	212.11	227.7	252.0	182.4	229.3	11.7	309.2	74.3
November	328.66	108.07	195.32	253.5	239.8	203.1	214.5	13.1	303.4	82.8
December	325.57	118.73	179.06	278.5	227.9	223.1	200.1	14.3	297.9	91.0

Months.	XXI.	XXII.	XXIII.	XXIV.	XXV.	XXVI.	XXVII.	XXVIII.	XXIX.	XXX.
	o	o	o	o	o	o	o	o	o	o
January	0.0	0.0	0.0	0.0	0.0	0.0	0.0	0.0	0.0	0.0
February	27.8	30.4	338.1	15.6	351.7	356.2	333.5	3.3	0.7	10.4
March	52.9	57.8	318.2	29.6	344.1	352.8	309.6	6.3	1.4	19.8
April	80.7	88.2	296.3	45.2	335.8	348.9	283.2	9.6	2.1	30.2
May	107.7	117.6	275.0	60.2	327.7	345.3	257.5	12.7	2.8	40.3
June	135.5	146.0	253.1	75.8	319.4	341.4	231.4	16.0	3.5	50.7
July	162.4	177.4	231.9	90.9	311.3	337.8	205.4	19.2	4.2	60.7
August	190.2	207.8	209.9	106.4	303.0	333.9	179.0	22.5	4.9	71.1
September	216.0	238.1	188.0	122.0	294.6	330.1	152.5	25.8	5.6	81.5
October	244.9	267.5	166.7	137.0	286.6	326.4	126.9	29.0	6.3	91.6
November	272.7	297.0	144.8	152.6	278.2	322.6	100.4	32.3	7.0	102.0
December	299.6	327.3	123.5	167.7	270.2	318.9	74.8	35.4	7.7	112.1

In Bissextile Years subtract one day from the date in the first two months.

TABLE III. — *Continued.*

FOR THE ARGUMENTS.

B. Variations of the Arguments for the different Months. The times are referred to the meridian of Washington.

Months.	XXXI.	XXXII.	XXXIII.	XXXIV.	XXXV.	XXXVI.	XXXVII.	XXXVIII	XXXIX.	XL.
January	0	0	0	0	0	0	0	0	0	0
February	33	347	25	349	42	20	340	336	45	18
March	63	334	48	330	80	38	322	315	85	33
April	96	321	73	328	122	58	302	291	130	51
May	128	308	98	318	163	78	283	267	173	68
June	161	294	123	307	205	98	263	244	217	85
July	192	281	147	296	245	117	243	220	260	102
August	225	268	173	285	287	137	223	197	305	120
September	258	254	198	274	330	157	203	173	350	137
October	290	241	222	264	10	177	184	150	33	154
November	323	228	247	253	52	197	164	126	77	172
December	355	215	272	242	93	216	145	102	121	189

Months.	XLI.	XLII.	XLIII.	XLIV.	XLV.	XLVI.	XLVII.	XLVIII.	XLIX.	
January	0	0	0	0	0	0	0	0	0	
February	15	40	324	30	343	25	49	333	337	
March	28	76	291	57	327	47	94	308	317	
April	43	116	255	87	310	71	143	281	294	
May	58	155	220	115	293	95	190	255	273	
June	73	195	184	145	275	120	239	228	250	
July	87	234	149	174	258	144	287	202	228	
August	102	274	113	204	241	168	336	175	206	
September	117	314	77	234	224	193	25	148	183	
October	131	353	42	262	207	217	73	121	161	
November	146	33	6	292	189	241	122	94	139	
December	161	72	331	321	172	265	169	68	117	

In Bissextile Years subtract one day from the date in the first two months.

TABLE III.— *Continued.*

FOR THE ARGUMENTS.

C. Variations of the Arguments for the different Days. The times are referred to the meridian of Washington.

Days.	I.	II.	III.	IV.	V.	VI.	VII.	VIII.	IX.	X.
	°	°	°	°	°	°	°	°	°	°
1	359.917	0.146	0.063	359.980	0.52	0.21	0.08	359.60	0.23	0.60
2	359.834	0.292	0.126	359.960	1.04	0.42	0.75	359.37	0.46	1.21
3	359.751	0.439	0.189	359.940	1.57	0.63	1.13	359.06	0.69	1.81
4	359.667	0.585	0.252	359.920	2.09	0.84	1.50	358.75	0.92	2.42
5	359.584	0.731	0.316	359.900	2.61	1.05	1.88	358.44	1.15	3.02
6	359.501	0.877	0.379	359.880	3.13	1.26	2.25	358.12	1.38	3.63
7	359.418	1.023	0.442	359.860	3.65	1.47	2.63	357.81	1.61	4.23
8	359.335	1.170	0.505	359.840	4.17	1.67	3.00	357.50	1.83	4.84
9	359.252	1.316	0.568	359.820	4.70	1.88	3.38	357.19	2.06	5.44
10	359.169	1.462	0.631	359.800	5.22	2.09	3.76	356.88	2.29	6.05
20	358.338	2.924	1.262	359.600	10.43	4.19	7.51	353.75	4.59	12.10
30	357.508	4.386	1.893	359.400	15.65	6.28	11.27	350.63	6.88	18.14

Days.	XI.	XII.	XIII.	XIV.	XV.	XVI.	XVII.	XVIII.	XIX.	XX.
	°	°	°	°	°	°	°	°	°	°
1	359.90	0.36	359.46	0.8	359.6	0.7	359.5	0.0	359.8	0.3
2	359.79	0.71	358.92	1.7	359.2	1.3	359.0	0.1	359.6	0.5
3	359.69	1.07	358.37	2.5	358.8	2.0	358.6	0.1	359.4	0.8
4	359.59	1.42	357.83	3.3	358.4	2.7	358.1	0.2	359.3	1.1
5	359.49	1.78	357.29	4.2	358.0	3.3	357.6	0.2	359.1	1.4
6	359.38	2.13	356.75	5.0	357.6	4.0	357.1	0.3	358.9	1.6
7	359.28	2.49	356.21	5.8	357.2	4.7	356.7	0.3	358.7	1.9
8	359.18	2.84	355.66	6.7	356.8	5.3	356.2	0.3	358.5	2.2
9	359.07	3.20	355.12	7.5	356.4	6.0	355.7	0.4	358.3	2.5
10	358.97	3.56	354.58	8.3	356.0	6.7	355.2	0.4	358.1	2.7
20	357.94	7.11	349.17	16.7	352.1	13.4	350.4	0.9	356.3	5.4
30	356.91	10.67	343.75	25.0	348.1	12.0	345.6	1.3	354.2	8.2

Days.	XXI.	XXII.	XXIII.	XXIV.	XXV.	XXVI.	XXVII.	XXVIII.	XXIX.	XXX.
	°	°	°	°	°	°	°	°	°	°
1	0.9	1.0	359.3	0.5	359.7	359.9	359.1	0.1	0.0	0.3
2	1.8	2.0	358.6	1.0	359.5	359.8	358.3	0.2	0.1	0.7
3	2.7	2.9	357.9	1.5	359.2	359.6	357.4	0.3	0.1	1.0
4	3.6	3.9	357.2	2.0	358.9	359.5	356.6	0.4	0.1	1.3
5	4.5	4.9	356.5	2.5	358.7	359.4	355.7	0.5	0.1	1.7
6	5.4	5.9	355.8	3.0	358.4	359.3	354.9	0.6	0.1	2.0
7	6.3	6.9	355.0	3.5	358.1	359.1	354.0	0.7	0.2	2.4
8	7.2	7.8	354.3	4.0	357.9	359.0	353.2	0.9	0.2	2.7
9	8.2	8.8	353.6	4.5	357.6	358.9	352.3	1.0	0.2	3.0
10	9.0	9.8	352.9	5.0	357.3	358.8	351.5	1.1	0.2	3.4
20	17.9	19.6	345.8	10.0	354.6	357.5	342.9	2.1	0.5	6.7
30	26.9	29.4	338.8	15.1	351.9	356.3	334.4	3.2	0.7	10.1

TABLE III. — *Continued.*

FOR THE ARGUMENTS.

C. Variations of the Arguments for the different Days. The times are referred to the meridian of Washington.

Days.	XXXI.	XXXII.	XXXIII.	XXXIV.	XXXV.	XXXVI.	XXXVII.	XXXVIII	XXXIX.	XL.
	°	°	°	°	°	°	°	°	°	°
1	1	0	1	0	1	1	359	359	1	1
2	2	359	2	359	3	1	359	358	3	1
3	3	359	2	359	4	2	358	358	4	2
4	4	358	3	359	5	3	357	357	6	2
5	5	358	4	358	7	3	357	356	7	3
6	6	357	5	358	8	4	356	355	9	3
7.	7	357	6	358	9	5	355	355	10	4
8	8	357	7	357	11	5	355	354	12	4
9	9	356	7	357	12	6	354	353	13	5
10	11	356	8	356	14	6	354	352	14	6
20	21	351	16	353	27	13	347	345	29	11
30	32	347	24	349	41	19	341	337	43	17

Days.	XLI.	XLII.	XLIII.	XLIV.	XLV.	XLVI.	XLVII.	XLVIII.	XLIX.	
	°	°	°	°	°	°	°	°	°	
1	0	1	359	1	359	1	2	359	359	
2	1	3	358	2	359	2	3	358	359	
3	1	4	357	3	358	2	5	357	358	
4	2	5	355	4	358	3	6	357	357	
5	2	7	354	5	357	4	8	356	356	
6	3	8	353	6	357	5	10	355	356	
7	3	9	352	7	356	6	11	354	355	
8	4	10	351	8	356	6	13	353	354	
9	4	12	350	9	355	7	14	352	353	
10	5	13	348	10	354	8	16	351	353	
20	10	26	337	19	349	16	32	343	345	
30	14	39	325	29	343	24	48	334	338	

TABLE III. — *Concluded.*

FOR THE ARGUMENTS.

D. Variations of the Arguments for the different Hours. The times are referred to the meridian of Washington.

Hours.	I.	II.	III.	IV.	V.	VI.	VII.	VIII.	IX.	X.
	°	°	°	°	°	°	°	°	°	°
1	359.997	0.006	0.003	359.999	0.02	0.01	0.02	359.99	0.01	0.03
2	359.993	0.012	0.005	359.998	0.04	0.02	0.03	359.97	0.02	0.05
3	359.990	0.018	0.008	359.998	0.07	0.03	0.05	359.96	0.03	0.07
4	359.986	0.024	0.010	359.997	0.09	0.04	0.06	359.95	0.04	0.10
5	359.983	0.031	0.013	359.996	0.11	0.04	0.08	359.94	0.04	0.12
6	359.979	0.037	0.016	359.995	0.13	0.05	0.10	359.92	0.05	0.15
7	359.976	0.043	0.018	359.994	0.15	0.06	0.11	359.91	0.06	0.17
8	359.972	0.049	0.021	359.994	0.18	0.07	0.13	359.90	0.07	0.20
9	359.969	0.055	0.023	359.993	0.20	0.08	0.14	359.88	0.08	0.22
10	359.965	0.061	0.026	359.992	0.22	0.09	0.16	359.87	0.09	0.25
20	359.930	0.122	0.052	359.984	0.44	0.18	0.32	359.74	0.18	0.50

Hours.	XI.	XII.	XIII.	XIV.	XV.	XVI.	XVII.	XVIII.	XIX.	XX.
	°	°	°	°	°	°	°	°	°	°
1	0.00	0.02	359.98	0.0	0.0	0.0	0.0	0.0	0.0	0.0
2	359.99	0.03	359.95	0.1	0.0	0.1	0.0	0.0	0.0	0.0
3	359.99	0.04	359.93	0.1	359.9	0.1	359.9	0.0	0.0	0.0
4	359.98	0.06	359.91	0.1	359.9	0.1	359.9	0.0	0.0	0.0
5	359.98	0.07	359.88	0.2	359.9	0.1	359.9	0.0	0.0	0.1
6	359.98	0.09	359.86	0.2	359.9	0.2	359.9	0.0	359.9	0.1
7	359.97	0.10	359.84	0.2	359.9	0.2	359.9	0.0	359.9	0.1
8	359.97	0.12	359.82	0.3	359.9	0.2	359.8	0.0	359.9	0.1
9	359.96	0.13	359.79	0.3	359.8	0.3	359.8	0.0	359.9	0.1
10	359.96	0.15	359.77	0.4	359.8	0.3	359.8	0.0	359.9	0.1
20	359.92	0.30	359.54	0.7	359.7	0.6	359.6	0.0	359.8	0.2

Hours.	XXI.	XXII.	XXIII.	XXIV.	XXV.	XXVI.	XXVII.	XXVIII.	XXIX.	XXX.
	°	°	°	°	°	°	°	°	°	°
1	0.0	0.0	0.0	0.0	0.0	0.0	0.0	0.0	0.0	0.0
2	0.1	0.1	359.9	0.0	0.0	0.0	359.9	0.0	0.0	0.0
3	0.1	0.1	359.9	0.1	0.0	0.0	359.9	0.0	0.0	0.0
4	0.1	0.2	359.9	0.1	0.0	0.0	359.9	0.0	0.0	0.0
5	0.2	0.2	359.8	0.1	359.9	0.0	359.8	0.0	0.0	0.0
6	0.2	0.3	359.8	0.1	359.9	0.0	359.8	0.0	0.0	0.0
7	0.3	0.3	359.8	0.2	359.9	0.0	359.7	0.0	0.0	0.0
8	0.3	0.3	359.8	0.2	359.9	0.0	359.7	0.0	0.0	0.0
9	0.3	0.4	359.7	0.2	359.9	359.9	359.7	0.0	0.0	0.0
10	0.4	0.4	359.7	0.2	359.9	359.9	359.6	0.0	0.0	0.0
20	0.7	0.8	359.4	0.4	359.8	359.9	359.3	0.1	0.0	0.3

TABLE IV.

PERTURBATIONS OF THE CO-ORDINATES IN UNITS OF THE SIXTH DECIMAL.

Terms multiplied with t. Argument $= M$.

Arg.	ξ'	Diff.	η'	Diff.	ζ'	Diff.	Arg.	ξ'	Diff.	η'	Diff.	ζ'	Diff.
0	+10.37	+17·90	−833.64	+0·02	−8.63	−3·32	45	+585.90	+5·49	−465.98	+12·88	−129.21	−1·60
1	27.57	17·19	833.62	0·49	12.15	3·32	46	591.39	5·15	453.10	12·89	130.81	1·54
2	44.76	17·17	833.13	0·87	15.47	3·31	47	596.54	4·81	440.21	12·90	132.35	1·49
3	61.93	17·14	832.16	1·44	18.78	3·30	48	601.35	4·49	427.31	12·90	133.84	1·43
4	79.07	17·07	830.72	1·90	22.08	3·29	49	605.84	4·16	414.41	12·89	135.27	1·37
5	96.14	17·00	828.82	2·37	25.37	3·27	50	610.00	3·84	401.52	12·88	136.64	1·32
6	113.14	16·91	826.45	2·63	28.64	3·26	51	613.84	3·53	388.64	12·88	137.96	1·26
7	130.05	16·80	823.62	3·29	31.90	3·24	52	617.37	3·22	375.79	12·68	139.22	1·21
8	146.85	16·67	820.33	3·74	35.14	3·22	53	620.59	2·91	362.97	12·82	140.43	1·15
9	163.52	16·54	816.59	4·19	38.36	3·20	54	623.50	2·61	350.18	12·79	141.58	1·09
10	+180.06	+16·38	−812.40	+4·62	−41.56	−3·17	55	+626.11	+2·31	−337.43	+12·69	−142.67	−1·04
11	196.44	16·20	807.78	5·06	44.73	3·15	56	628.42	2·03	324.74	12·63	143.71	0·98
12	212.64	16·02	802.72	5·49	47.88	3·12	57	630.45	1·74	312.11	12·56	144.69	0·92
13	228.66	15·82	797.24	5·90	51.00	3·09	58	632.19	1·47	299.55	12·49	145.61	0·87
14	244.48	15·62	791.34	6·30	54.09	3·07	59	633.66	1·20	287.06	12·41	146.49	0·81
15	260.10	15·39	785.04	6·70	57.16	3·04	60	634.86	0·93	274.65	12·32	147.29	0·76
16	275.49	15·14	778.34	7·09	60.20	3·00	61	635.79	0·67	262.33	12·23	148.05	0·71
17	290.63	14·90	771.25	7·46	63.20	2·97	62	636.46	0·41	250.10	12·14	148.76	0·65
18	305.53	14·63	763.79	7·46	66.17	2·93	63	636.87	+0·16	237.96	12·04	149.41	0·60
19	320.16	14·36	755.96	7·83	69.10	2·89	64	637.03	−0·07	225.92	11·94	150.01	0·55
20	+334.52	+14·08	−747.78	+8·52	−71.99	−2·86	65	+636.96	−0·32	−213.98	+11·84	−150.56	−0·49
21	348.60	13·79	739.26	8·85	74.85	2·82	66	636.64	0·54	202.14	11·74	151.05	0·44
22	362.39	13·48	730.41	9·17	77.67	2·77	67	636.10	0·77	190.40	11·62	151.49	0·39
23	375.87	13·17	721.24	9·47	80.44	2·74	68	635.33	0·98	178.78	11·52	151.88	0·34
24	389.04	12·85	711.77	9·47	83.18	2·69	69	634.35	1·20	167.26	11·52	152.22	0·29
25	401.89	12·53	702.00	9·77	85.87	2·66	70	633.15	1·40	155.86	11·40	152.51	0·23
26	414.42	12·20	691.96	10·04	88.52	2·60	71	631.75	1·40	144.59	11·27	152.74	0·19
27	426.62	11·86	681.65	10·31	91.12	2·66	72	630.14	1·61	133.44	11·15	152.93	0·13
28	438.48	11·52	671.09	10·56	93.67	2·51	73	628.34	1·80	122.42	11·02	153.06	0·09
29	450.00	11·17	660.30	10·79	96.18	2·46	74	626.34	2·00	111.52	10·90	153.15	0·03
30	+461.17	+10·82	−649.28	+11·23	−98.64	−2·41	75	+624.16	−2·36	−100.76	+10·63	−153.18	+0·02
31	471.99	10·46	638.05	11·42	101.05	2·35	76	621.80	2·53	90.13	10·50	153.16	0·06
32	482.45	10·10	626.63	11·60	103.40	2·31	77	619.27	2·71	79.63	10·36	153.10	0·11
33	492.55	9·74	615.03	11·78	105.71	2·25	78	616.56	2·87	69.27	10·23	152.99	0·15
34	502.29	9·39	603.25	11·93	107.96	2·20	79	613.69	3·02	59.04	10·10	152.84	0·20
35	511.68	9·03	591.32	12·08	110.16	2·15	80	610.67	3·18	48.94	9·97	152.64	0·26
36	520.71	8·67	579.24	12·22	112.31	2·09	81	607.49	3·33	38.97	9·83	152.39	0·29
37	529.38	8·31	567.02	12·33	114.40	2·04	82	604.16	3·48	29.14	9·68	152.10	0·34
38	537.69	7·96	554.69	12·44	116.44	2·04	83	600.68	3·61	19.46	9·55	151.76	0·38
39	545.65	7·60	542.25	12·64	118.43	1·03	84	597.07	3·75	9.91	9·41	151.38	0·43
40	+553.25	+7·24	−529.71	+12·62	−120.36	−1·98	85	+593.32	−3·87	−0.50	+9·26	−150.95	+0·47
41	560.49	6·68	517.09	12·70	122.24	1·83	86	589.45	4·00	+8.76	9·13	150.48	0·51
42	567.37	6·62	504.39	12·78	124.07	1·77	87	585.45	4·13	17.89	8·97	149.97	0·56
43	573.89	6·18	491.63	12·80	125.84	1·71	88	581.32	4·24	26.86	8·87	149.41	0·60
44	580.07	5·89	478.83	12·86	127.55	1·66	89	577.08	4·35	35.73	8·71	148.81	0·64
45	+585.90		−465.98		−129.21		90	+572.73		+44.44		−148.17	

TABLE IV. — *Continued.*

PERTURBATIONS OF THE CO-ORDINATES IN UNITS OF THE SIXTH DECIMAL.

Terms multiplied with *t*. Argument = *M*.

Arg.	ξ'	Diff.	η'	Diff.	ζ'	Diff.	Arg.	ξ'	Diff.	η'	Diff.	ζ'	Diff.
90	+572.73	−4.46	+44.44	+8.57	−148.17	−0.69	135	+309.51	−6.59	+305.43	+3.27	−85.39	+1.96
91	568.27	4.56	53.01	8.44	147.48	0.72	136	302.92	6.60	308.70	3.18	83.43	1.97
92	563.71	4.67	61.45	8.29	146.76	0.76	137	296.32	6.61	311.88	3.09	81.46	1.99
93	559.04	4.76	69.74	8.16	146.00	0.80	138	289.71	6.61	314.97	3.09	79.47	1.99
94	554.28	4.86	77.90	8.02	145.20	0.84	139	283.09	6.62	317.97	3.00	77.47	2.00
95	549.42	4.94	85.92	7.89	144.36	0.89	140	276.46	6.63	320.88	2.91	75.45	2.02
96	544.48	5.04	93.81	7.75	143.48	0.91	141	269.83	6.63	323.70	2.82	73.41	2.04
97	539.44	5.12	101.56	7.62	142.57	0.93	142	263.19	6.64	326.43	2.73	71.36	2.05
98	534.32	5.20	109.18	7.48	141.62	0.95	143	256.54	6.65	329.08	2.65	69.29	2.07
99	529.12	5.29	116.66	7.35	140.64	0.98	144	249.89	6.65	331.64	2.56	67.21	2.08
100	+523.81	−5.36	+124.01	+7.22	−139.62	−1.02	145	+243.24	−6.65	+334.11	+2.47	−65.12	+2.09
101	518.44	5.42	131.23	7.08	138.56	1.06	146	236.59	6.65	336.49	2.38	63.02	2.10
102	513.06	5.49	138.31	6.95	137.47	1.09	147	229.94	6.65	338.79	2.30	60.90	2.12
103	507.58	5.55	145.26	6.82	136.34	1.13	148	223.28	6.66	341.01	2.22	58.77	2.13
104	502.03	5.61	152.08	6.69	135.18	1.16	149	216.62	6.66	343.14	2.13	56.63	2.14
105	496.42	5.67	158.77	6.56	133.98	1.20	150	209.96	6.66	345.20	2.06	54.48	2.15
106	490.75	5.73	165.33	6.44	132.75	1.23	151	203.29	6.67	347.18	1.98	52.32	2.16
107	485.02	5.78	171.77	6.31	131.48	1.27	152	196.62	6.67	349.08	1.90	50.15	2.17
108	479.24	5.83	178.08	6.19	130.19	1.29	153	189.95	6.67	350.90	1.82	47.97	2.18
109	473.41	5.89	184.27	6.07	128.87	1.32	154	183.28	6.67	352.64	1.74	45.78	2.19
110	+467.52	−5.93	+190.34	+5.95	−127.52	−1.35	155	+176.61	−6.67	+354.30	+1.66	−43.59	+2.19
111	461.59	5.98	196.29	5.83	126.14	1.38	156	169.94	6.67	355.89	1.59	41.38	2.21
112	455.61	6.02	202.12	5.71	124.73	1.41	157	163.27	6.66	357.40	1.51	39.16	2.22
113	449.59	6.07	207.83	5.59	123.30	1.43	158	156.61	6.67	358.84	1.44	36.94	2.22
114	443.52	6.10	213.42	5.47	121.83	1.47	159	149.94	6.66	360.20	1.36	34.71	2.23
115	437.42	6.14	218.89	5.35	120.33	1.50	160	143.28	6.67	361.48	1.28	32.47	2.24
116	431.28	6.18	224.24	5.24	118.81	1.52	161	136.61	6.66	362.69	1.21	30.23	2.24
117	425.10	6.21	229.48	5.12	117.26	1.55	162	129.95	6.66	363.83	1.14	27.98	2.25
118	418.89	6.25	234.60	5.01	115.68	1.58	163	123.29	6.67	364.90	1.07	25.73	2.25
119	412.64	6.28	239.61	4.90	114.08	1.60	164	116.62	6.66	365.90	1.00	23.47	2.26
120	+406.36	−6.31	+244.51	+4.77	−112.45	−1.63	165	+109.96	−6.66	+366.82	+0.85	−21.21	+2.27
121	400.05	6.33	249.28	4.71	110.80	1.65	166	103.30	6.65	367.67	0.78	18.94	2.27
122	393.72	6.36	253.99	4.59	109.12	1.68	167	96.65	6.65	368.45	0.71	16.67	2.27
123	387.36	6.38	258.57	4.47	107.42	1.70	168	90.00	6.64	369.16	0.64	14.40	2.27
124	380.98	6.41	263.04	4.36	105.69	1.73	169	83.36	6.64	369.80	0.58	12.13	2.28
125	374.57	6.43	267.40	4.26	103.95	1.74	170	76.72	6.64	370.38	0.50	9.85	2.28
126	368.14	6.45	271.66	4.15	102.18	1.77	171	70.08	6.63	370.88	0.43	7.57	2.28
127	361.69	6.46	275.81	4.05	100.39	1.79	172	63.45	6.62	371.31	0.37	5.29	2.29
128	355.23	6.48	279.86	3.95	98.59	1.80	173	56.83	6.63	371.68	0.29	3.00	2.28
129	348.75	6.50	283.81	3.84	96.76	1.83	174	50.20	6.63	371.97	0.22	−0.72	2.29
130	+342.25	−6.52	+287.65	+3.75	−94.91	−1.85	175	+43.57	−6.63	+372.19	+0.16	+1.57	+2.28
131	335.73	6.53	291.40	3.65	93.05	1.86	176	36.94	6.63	372.35	0.09	3.85	2.29
132	329.20	6.55	295.05	3.55	91.16	1.89	177	30.31	6.62	372.44	0.02	6.14	2.29
133	322.65	6.56	298.60	3.46	89.25	1.91	178	23.69	6.62	372.46	−0.05	8.43	2.28
134	316.09	6.58	302.06	3.37	87.33	1.92	179	17.07	6.62	372.41	−0.11	10.71	2.28
135	+309.51		+305.43		−85.39	1.94	180	+10.45		+372.30		+12.99	

TABLE IV. — *Continued.*

PERTURBATIONS OF THE CO-ORDINATES IN UNITS OF THE ·SIXTH DECIMAL.

Terms multiplied with t. Argument $= M$.

Arg.	ξ'	Diff.	η'	Diff.	ζ'	Diff.	Arg.	ξ'	Diff.	η'	Diff.	ζ'	Diff.
180	+ 10.45	−6.61	+372.30	−0.18	+ 12.99	+2.28	225	−281.71	−6.28	+294.58	−3.48	+106.59	+1.73
181	+ 3.84	6.61	372.12	0.25	15.27	2.27	226	287.99	6.27	291.10	3.57	108.32	1.71
182	− 2.77	6.60	371.87	0.32	17.54	2.27	227	294.26	6.26	287.53	3.66	110.03	1.69
183	9.37	6.60	371.55	0.39	19.81	2.27	228	300.52	6.25	283.87	3.74	111.72	1.67
184	15.97	6.60	371.16	0.45	22.08	2.26	229	306.77	6.23	280.13	3.84	113.39	1.64
185	22.57	6.59	370.71	0.52	24.34	2.26	230	313.00	6.21	276.29	3.92	115.03	1.62
186	29.16	6.58	370.19	0.59	26.60	2.25	231	319.21	6.19	272.37	4.01	116.65	1.59
187	35.74	6.58	369.60	0.66	28.85	2.25	232	325.40	6.17	268.36	4.11	118.24	1.57
188	42.32	6.58	368.94	0.72	31.10	2.24	233	331.57	6.15	264.25	4.21	119.81	1.57
189	48.90	6.57	368.21	0.80	33.34	2.23	234	337.72	6.13	260.04	4.30	121.36	1.53
190	− 55.47	−6.57	+367.41	−0.86	+ 35.57	+2.23	235	−343.85	−6.10	+255.74	−4.39	+122.89	+1.50
191	62.04	6.56	366.55	0.93	37.80	2.22	236	349.95	6.08	251.35	4.49	124.39	1.47
192	68.60	6.57	365.62	0.99	40.02	2.21	237	356.03	6.05	246.86	4.59	125.86	1.44
193	75.17	6.56	364.63	1.07	42.23	2.21	238	362.08	6.02	242.27	4.69	127.30	1.42
194	81.73	6.55	363.56	1.13	44.44	2.20	239	368.10	6.00	237.58	4.79	128.72	1.39
195	88.28	6.55	362.43	1.20	46.64	2.19	240	374.10	5.97	232.79	4.89	130.11	1.36
196	94.83	6.54	361.23	1.28	48.83	2.18	241	380.07	5.94	227.90	4.99	131.47	1.34
197	101.37	6.54	359.95	1.34	51.01	2.17	242	386.01	5.90	222.91	5.09	132.81	1.30
198	107.91	6.53	358.61	1.34	53.18	2.17	243	391.91	5.90	217.82	5.09	134.11	1.30
199	114.44	6.52	357.20	1.41	55.34	2.16	244	397.78	5.87	212.63	5.19	135.38	1.27
200	−120.96	−6.52	+355.71	−1.55	+ 57.48	+2.14	245	−403.62	−5.80	+207.33	−5.41	+136.62	+1.21
201	127.48	6.51	354.16	1.63	59.62	2.13	246	409.42	5.77	201.92	5.52	137.83	1.18
202	133.99	6.51	352.53	1.69	61.75	2.11	247	415.19	5.72	196.40	5.63	139.01	1.14
203	140.59	6.50	350.84	1.77	63.86	2.10	248	420.91	5.69	190.77	5.74	140.15	1.12
204	147.00	6.50	349.07	1.84	65.96	2.09	249	426.60	5.65	185.03	5.85	141.27	1.08
205	153.50	6.50	347.23	1.91	68.05	2.08	250	432.25	5.60	179.18	5.96	142.35	1.05
206	160.00	6.49	345.32	1.99	70.13	2.06	251	437.85	5.55	173.22	6.08	143.40	1.01
207	166.49	6.48	343.33	1.99	72.19	2.06	252	443.40	5.53	167.14	6.08	144.41	1.01
208	172.97	6.48	341.27	2.06	74.24	2.05	253	448.90	5.50	160.95	6.19	145.39	0.98
209	179.45	6.47	339.14	2.13	76.28	2.04	254	454.35	5.45	154.65	6.30	146.34	0.95
210	−185.92	−6.45	+336.94	−2.27	+ 78.30	+2.01	255	−459.75	−5.34	+148.23	−6.54	+147.25	+0.88
211	192.37	6.45	334.67	2.34	80.31	1.99	256	465.09	5.29	141.69	6.60	148.13	0.84
212	198.82	6.43	332.33	2.42	82.30	1.97	257	470.38	5.22	135.03	6.78	148.97	0.80
213	205.25	6.42	329.91	2.50	84.27	1.96	258	475.60	5.16	128.25	6.91	149.77	0.70
214	211.67	6.41	327.41	2.58	86.23	1.94	259	480.76	5.09	121.34	7.03	150.53	0.73
215	218.08	6.41	324.83	2.65	88.17	1.92	260	485.85	5.03	114.31	7.15	151.26	0.69
216	224.49	6.41	322.18	2.74	90.09	1.91	261	490.88	5.03	107.16	7.15	151.95	0.65
217	230.89	6.40	319.44	2.83	92.00	1.89	262	495.83	4.96	99.88	7.28	152.60	0.61
218	237.29	6.40	316.61	2.90	93.89	1.87	263	500.71	4.88	92.48	7.40	153.21	0.57
219	243.68	6.39	313.71	2.99	95.76	1.86	264	505.52	4.81	84.95	7.53	153.78	0.53
220	−250.06	−6.36	+310.72	−3.06	+ 97.62	+1.83	265	−510.25	−4.65	+ 77.30	−7.78	+154.31	+0.48
221	256.42	6.35	307.66	3.15	99.45	1.62	266	514.90	4.56	69.52	7.90	154.79	0.45
222	262.77	6.33	304.51	3.23	101.27	1.79	267	519.46	4.47	61.62	8.03	155.24	0.41
223	269.10	6.31	301.28	3.31	103.06	1.76	268	523.93	4.38	53.59	8.16	155.65	0.36
224	275.41	6.30	297.97	3.31	104.84	1.75	269	528.31	4.28	45.43	8.16	156.01	0.36
225	−281.71	−6.30	+294.58	−3.39	+106.59	+1.75	270	−532.59	−4.28	+ 37.14	−8.29	+156.33	+0.33

TABLE IV. — *Continued.*

PERTURBATIONS OF THE CO-ORDINATES IN UNITS OF THE SIXTH DECIMAL.

Terms multiplied with t. Argument $= M$.

Arg.	ξ'	Diff.	η'	Diff.	ζ'	Diff.	Arg.	ξ'	Diff.	η'	Diff.	ζ'	Diff.
270	−532.59	−4.19	+37.14	−8.43	+156.33	+0.28	315	−549.99	+5.44	−458.42	−12.64	+120.33	−1.99
271	536.78	−4.08	28.71	−8.57	156.61	0.23	316	544.55	5.67	471.06	12.61	118.34	2.05
272	540.86	4.08	20.14	8.57	156.84	0.23	317	538.78	6.11	483.67	12.58	116.29	2.10
273	544.83	3.97	11.45	8.69	157.03	0.19	318	532.67	6.46	496.25	12.58	114.19	2.16
274	548.69	3.86	+2.62	8.83	157.17	0.14	319	526.21	6.46	508.79	12.54	112.03	2.16
275	552.43	3.74	−6.34	8.96	157.27	0.10	320	519.40	6.81	521.27	12.48	109.83	2.20
276	556.05	3.62	15.43	9.09	157.32	0.05	321	512.25	7.13	533.69	12.42	107.57	2.26
277	559.55	3.60	24.66	9.23	157.33	+0.01	322	504.74	7.51	546.03	12.34	105.26	2.31
278	562.91	3.30	34.02	9.36	157.29	−0.04	323	496.88	7.86	558.27	12.24	102.91	2.35
279	566.14	3.23	43.51	9.49	157.20	−0.09	324	488.67	8.21	570.42	12.15	100.51	2.40
		3.09		9.62		0.14			8.37		12.03		2.43
280	−569.23	−2.95	−53.13	−9.76	+157.06	+0.14	325	−480.10	+8.93	−582.45	−11.90	+98.06	−2.49
281	572.18	2.86	62.89	9.76	156.88	−0.18	326	471.17	9.29	594.35	11.76	95.57	2.54
282	574.98	2.65	72.77	9.88	156.65	0.23	327	461.88	9.65	606.11	11.61	93.03	2.59
283	577.63	2.50	82.78	10.01	156.37	0.29	328	452.23	10.00	617.72	11.43	90.44	2.63
284	580.13	2.34	92.93	10.13	156.05	0.32	329	442.23	10.36	629.15	11.27	87.81	2.67
285	582.47	2.17	103.20	10.27	155.68	0.37	330	431.87	10.72	640.42	11.08	85.14	2.72
286	584.64	2.00	113.60	10.40	155.26	0.42	331	421.15	11.00	651.50	10.87	82.42	2.75
287	586.64	1.82	124.13	10.53	154.79	0.47	332	410.09	11.41	662.37	10.66	79.67	2.80
288	588.46	1.64	134.78	10.65	154.27	0.52	333	398.68	11.75	673.03	10.42	76.87	2.84
289	590.10	1.64	145.56	10.78	153.69	0.58	334	386.93	12.06	683.45	10.19	74.03	2.88
		1.45		10.91		0.62			12.06		10.19		2.88
290	−591.55	−1.25	−156.47	−11.02	+153.07	−0.68	335	−374.84	+12.42	−693.63	−9.92	+71.15	−2.91
291	592.80	1.05	167.49	11.14	152.33	0.73	336	362.42	12.71	703.55	9.68	68.24	2.95
292	593.85	0.85	178.63	11.25	151.66	0.78	337	349.69	13.06	713.20	9.36	65.29	2.98
293	594.70	0.64	189.88	11.36	150.88	0.83	338	336.62	13.37	722.56	9.07	62.31	3.02
294	595.34	0.43	201.24	11.47	150.05	0.83	339	323.25	13.68	731.63	8.76	59.29	3.05
295	595.77	0.43	212.71	11.57	149.17	0.88	340	309.57	13.97	740.39	8.76	56.21	3.05
296	595.98	−0.21	224.28	11.68	148.23	0.94	341	295.60	14.27	748.83	8.44	53.17	3.07
297	595.96	+0.02	235.96	11.68	147.24	0.99	342	281.33	14.27	756.93	8.10	50.07	3.10
298	595.71	0.25	247.74	11.78	146.20	1.04	343	266.78	14.55	764.64	7.73	46.94	3.13
299	595.22	0.49	259.61	11.87	145.10	1.10	344	251.97	14.81	772.06	7.39	43.79	3.15
		0.74		11.96		1.15			15.07		7.01		3.18
300	−594.48	+0.99	−271.57	−12.06	+143.95	−1.20	345	−236.90	+15.32	−779.07	−6.60	+40.61	−3.20
301	593.49	1.25	283.63	12.15	142.75	1.25	346	221.58	15.54	785.67	6.27	37.41	3.23
302	592.24	1.51	295.78	12.22	141.50	1.30	347	206.04	15.76	791.94	5.84	34.18	3.24
303	590.73	1.78	308.00	12.28	140.20	1.36	348	190.28	15.96	797.78	5.43	30.94	3.27
304	588.95	2.06	320.28	12.37	138.84	1.41	349	174.32	16.15	803.21	5.01	27.67	3.28
305	586.89	2.33	332.63	12.41	137.43	1.47	350	158.17	16.32	808.22	4.58	24.39	3.29
306	584.56	2.63	345.04	12.47	135.96	1.53	351	141.85	16.48	812.80	4.14	21.10	3.30
307	581.93	2.92	357.51	12.52	134.43	1.58	352	125.36	16.62	816.94	3.69	17.80	3.32
308	579.01	3.21	370.03	12.56	132.85	1.63	353	108.74	16.76	820.63	3.69	14.48	3.32
309	575.80	3.51	382.59	12.60	131.22	1.66	354	91.98	16.76	823.87	3.24	11.16	3.33
		3.51		12.60		1.66			16.87		2.78		3.33
310	−572.29	+3.83	−395.19	−12.62	+129.53	−1.74	355	−75.11	+16.97	−826.65	−2.35	+7.83	−3.33
311	568.46	4.13	407.81	12.64	127.79	1.79	356	58.14	17.05	829.00	1.86	4.50	3.34
312	564.33	4.45	420.45	12.66	126.00	1.84	357	41.09	17.05	830.86	1.39	+1.16	3.34
313	559.88	4.78	433.11	12.65	124.16	1.89	358	23.98	17.11	832.25	0.93	2.17	3.33
314	555.10	4.78	445.76	12.65	122.27	1.89	359	−6.83	17.15	833.18	0.46	5.50	3.33
315	−549.99	+5.11	−458.42	−12.66	+120.33	−1.94	360	+10.37	+17.20	−833.64	−0.46	−8.83	−3.33

TABLE IV.— *Continued.*

PERTURBATIONS OF THE CO-ORDINATES IN UNITS OF THE SIXTH DECIMAL.

ARGUMENT I.

Arg.	ξ'	Diff.	η'	Diff.	ζ'	Diff.	Arg.	ξ'	Diff.	η'	Diff.	ζ'	Diff.
0	−3930	+96	+2377	+182	+17	−6	45	+4374	+160	+3666	−149	−256	−2
1	2834	103	2559	178	11	6	46	4534	154	3507	165	259	2
2	3731	112	2737	174	+5	6	47	4688	148	3342	172	260	1
3	3619	119	2911	170	−2	7	48	4836	140	3170	178	261	1
4	3500	126	3091	165	9	7	49	4976	132	2992	184	262	1
5	3374	133	3246	160	15	6	50	5108	125	2808	189	263	−1
6	3241	141	3406	154	22	7	51	5233	117	2619	195	263	0
7	3100	147	3569	149	30	8	52	5350	110	2424	199	263	0
8	2953	153	3700	143	37	7	53	5460	100	2225	204	263	0
9	2800	160	3852	137	44	7	54	5560	93	2021	209	263	+1
10	−2640	+166	+3989	+131	−51	−8	55	+5653	+84	+1812	−211	−262	+1
11	2474	171	4120	124	59	7	56	5737	75	1601	216	261	1
12	2303	177	4244	116	66	8	57	5812	66	1385	219	260	1
13	2126	182	4360	110	74	7	58	5878	57	1167	221	258	2
14	1944	187	4470	102	81	8	59	5935	48	946	223	256	2
15	1757	192	4572	95	89	7	60	5983	39	723	225	254	2
16	1565	196	4667	87	96	8	61	6022	30	498	226	252	2
17	1369	200	4754	78	104	7	62	6052	20	272	226	249	3
18	1169	203	4832	71	111	8	63	6072	12	+44	228	246	3
19	966	206	4903	62	119	7	64	6084	+2	−184	229	243	3
20	−760	+210	+4965	+64	−126	−8	65	+6086	−8	−413	−228	−239	+4
21	550	212	5019	45	134	7	66	6078	17	641	228	235	4
22	338	214	5064	37	141	7	67	6061	26	860	227	231	4
23	−124	217	5101	27	148	7	68	6035	35	1096	227	227	4
24	+93	217	5128	19	155	7	69	6000	35	1322	226	223	4
25	310	219	5147	+10	162	7	70	5956	44	1546	224	218	5
26	529	219	5157	0	168	6	71	5903	53	1768	222	213	5
27	748	218	5157	−9	175	7	72	5841	62	1988	220	208	5
28	967	220	5149	18	181	6	73	5770	71	2205	217	202	5
29	1187	219	5131	26	188	7	74	5691	79	2418	213	197	6
30	+1406	+218	+5105	−36	−194	−6	75	+5604	−96	−2628	−207	−191	+6
31	1624	217	5069	44	200	5	76	5508	103	2835	202	185	6
32	1841	216	5025	54	205	6	77	5405	112	3037	198	179	6
33	2056	213	4971	62	211	6	78	5293	119	3235	193	173	6
34	2269	211	4909	71	216	6	79	5174	126	3428	188	167	6
35	2480	209	4838	80	221	5	80	5048	133	3616	183	160	7
36	2688	208	4758	89	226	4	81	4915	140	3799	177	153	6
37	2892	201	4669	97	230	4	82	4775	146	3976	172	147	7
38	3093	198	4572	106	234	4	83	4629	153	4148	165	140	7
39	3291	193	4466	114	238	4	84	4476	159	4313	160	133	7
40	+3484	+198	+4352	−122	−242	−3	85	+4317	−164	−4473	−152	−126	+8
41	3672	184	4230	129	245	3	86	4153	170	4625	147	118	8
42	3856	178	4101	138	248	3	87	3983	175	4772	139	110	7
43	4034	173	3963	145	251	3	88	3808	179	4911	132	103	7
44	4207	167	3818	152	254	2	89	3629	184	5043	126	96	7
45	+4374		+3666		−256		90	+3445		−5169		−89	+7

TABLE IV. — *Continued.*

PERTURBATIONS OF THE CO-ORDINATES IN UNITS OF THE SIXTH DECIMAL.

ARGUMENT I.

Arg.	y'	Diff.	η'	Diff.	ζ	Diff.	Arg.	y'	Diff.	η'	Diff.	ζ	Diff.
90	+3445		-5169		-89		135	-4688		-3586		+238	
91	3257	-189	5247	-118	81	+8	136	4785	-97	3434	+152	244	+6
92	3065	192	5398	111	73	8	137	4876	91	3280	154	250	6
93	2870	195	5501	103	66	7	138	4962	86	3124	156	255	5
94	2671	199	5597	96	58	8	139	5042	80	2966	158	261	6
95	2470	201	5645	88	50	8	140	5116	74	2806	160	267	6
96	2267	203	5765	80	42	8	141	5185	69	2646	160	272	5
97	2061	206	5838	73	35	7	142	5248	63	2484	162	277	5
98	1853	208	5903	65	27	8	143	5305	57	2322	162	283	6
99	1643	210	5961	58	19	8	144	5357	52	2158	164	288	5
		210		49		8			46		163		5
100	+1433		-6010		-11		145	-5403		-1995		+293	
101	1221	-211	6052	-42	-3	+8	146	5444	-41	1831	+164	298	+5
102	1009	212	6086	34	+5	8	147	5479	35	1667	164	303	5
103	796	213	6113	27	12	7	148	5509	30	1503	164	307	4
104	584	212	6131	18	20	8	149	5533	24	1339	164	312	5
105	372	212	6142	11	28	8	150	5552	19	1175	164	316	4
106	+160	212	6146	-4	36	8	151	5566	14	1012	163	321	5
107	-51	211	6142	+4	43	7	152	5575	9	850	162	325	4
108	261	210	6131	11	51	8	153	5579	-4	689	161	329	4
109	469	208	6113	18	59	8	154	5577	+2	528	161	332	3
		207		26		7			6		159		4
110	-676		-6087		+66		155	-5571		-369		+336	
111	881	-205	6055	+32	74	+8	156	5560	11	212	+157	340	+4
112	1083	202	6016	39	82	8	157	5544	16	-56	156	343	3
113	1283	200	5970	46	89	7	158	5524	20	+99	155	346	3
114	1481	198	5917	53	97	8	159	5499	25	252	153	349	3
115	1675	194	5857	60	104	7	160	5470	29	404	152	352	3
116	1867	192	5792	65	111	7	161	5437	33	553	149	355	3
117	2055	188	5720	72	119	8	162	5399	38	700	147	358	3
118	2240	185	5642	78	126	7	163	5358	41	845	145	360	2
119	2421	181	5558	84	133	7	164	5312	46	986	143	362	2
		177		89		7			49		140		2
120	-2598		-5469		+140		165	-5263		+1129		+364	
121	2771	-173	5374	+95	147	+7	166	5210	+53	1266	+138	366	+2
122	2940	169	5274	100	154	7	167	5153	57	1402	136	367	1
123	3104	164	5169	105	161	7	168	5093	60	1535	133	369	2
124	3264	160	5059	110	168	7	169	5030	63	1665	130	370	1
125	3419	155	4944	115	175	7	170	4964	66	1793	128	371	1
126	3570	151	4825	119	181	0	171	4894	70	1917	124	371	0
127	3715	145	4701	124	188	7	172	4821	73	2039	122	372	+1
128	3855	140	4574	127	194	6	173	4746	75	2158	119	372	0
129	3990	135	4442	132	201	7	174	4668	78	2275	117	372	0
		130		135		6			81		113		0
130	-4120		-4307		+207		175	-4587		+2388		+372	
131	4245	-125	4169	+138	214	+7	176	4504	+83	2498	+110	371	-1
132	4364	119	4028	141	220	6	177	4418	86	2606	108	370	1
133	4478	114	3883	145	226	8	178	4330	88	2710	101	369	1
134	4586	108	3736	147	232	6	179	4240	90	2812	102	368	1
135	-4688	-102	-3586	+150	+238	+6	180	-4148	+92	+2910	+98	+366	-2

TABLE IV. — *Continued.*

PERTURBATIONS OF THE CO-ORDINATES IN UNITS OF THE SIXTH DECIMAL.

ARGUMENT I.

Arg.	ξ'	Diff.	η'	Diff.	ζ'	Diff.	Arg.	ξ'	Diff.	η'	Diff.	ζ'	Diff.
180	−4146	+94	+2910	+95	+366	−2	225	+988	+120	+4377	−31	+26	−12
181	4054	96	3005	92	364	2	226	1108	120	4346	35	14	12
182	3958	96	3097	92	362	2	227	1228	119	4311	38	+3	12
183	3860	98	3187	90	360	2	228	1347	119	4273	39	−9	12
184	3761	99	3273	86	357	3	229	1466	119	4232	41	20	11
185	3669	101	3356	83	354	3	230	1585	117	4188	44	31	11
186	3557	103	3436	80	350	4	231	1702	117	4141	47	42	11
187	3453	104	3513	77	347	3	232	1819	116	4090	51	53	11
188	3348	105	3587	74	343	4	233	1935	115	4036	54	64	11
189	3242	106	3658	71	339	4	234	2050	114	3979	57	75	11
		107		68		5			114		61		11
190	−3135	+109	+3726	+65	+334	−4	235	+2164	+113	+3918	−64	−86	−10
191	3026	109	3791	62	330	5	236	2277	111	3854	67	96	11
192	2917	111	3853	60	325	5	237	2388	110	3787	71	107	11
193	2806	111	3913	56	319	6	238	2498	109	3716	74	117	10
194	2695	113	3969	54	314	5	239	2607	107	3642	77	127	10
195	2582	113	4023	51	308	6	240	2714	106	3565	81	137	10
196	2469	113	4074	48	302	8	241	2820	103	3484	84	147	10
197	2356	113	4122	46	295	7	242	2923	102	3400	87	156	9
198	2241	115	4168	42	288	7	243	3025	100	3313	91	166	10
199	2126	115	4210	40	281	7	244	3125	98	3222	94	175	9
		115		40		7			98		94		8
200	−2011	+117	+4250	+37	+274	−8	245	+3223	+95	+3128	−98	−183	−9
201	1894	116	4287	35	266	8	246	3318	93	3030	101	192	8
202	1778	118	4322	32	258	8	247	3411	90	2929	104	200	8
203	1660	117	4354	29	250	8	248	3501	88	2825	107	208	7
204	1543	119	4383	27	242	8	249	3589	85	2718	110	215	8
205	1424	118	4410	24	233	9	250	3674	82	2608	113	223	7
206	1306	119	4434	21	225	8	251	3756	79	2495	116	230	7
207	1187	119	4455	19	216	9	252	3835	76	2379	120	236	6
208	1068	120	4474	16	206	10	253	3911	73	2259	122	243	7
209	948	120	4490	14	197	9	254	3984	69	2137	125	248	5
		120		14		10			69		125		6
210	−828	+120	+4504	+11	+187	−10	255	+4053	+66	+2012	−128	−254	−5
211	708	121	4515	8	177	10	256	4119	61	1884	131	259	5
212	587	120	4523	5	167	10	257	4180	58	1753	133	264	4
213	467	121	4528	3	157	10	258	4238	54	1620	136	268	4
214	346	121	4531	+3	147	10	259	4292	50	1484	138	272	4
215	225	121	4531	0	136	11	260	4342	46	1346	139	276	4
216	−103	122	4528	−3	126	10	261	4388	42	1206	140	279	3
217	+18	121	4523	5	115	11	262	4430	37	1063	143	282	3
218	140	122	4515	8	104	11	263	4467	32	918	145	285	3
219	261	121	4504	11	93	11	264	4499	27	772	146	287	2
		121		14		11			27		148		1
220	+382	+122	+4490	−16	+82	−11	265	+4526	+23	+624	−150	−288	−1
221	504	121	4474	20	71	11	266	4549	17	474	150	290	1
222	625	121	4454	20	59	12	267	4566	13	322	152	291	1
223	746	121	4431	23	48	11	268	4579	7	170	154	291	0
224	867	121	4406	25	37	11	269	4586	2	+16	155	291	0
225	+988	+121	+4377	−29	+26	−11	270	+4588		−139	155	−291	0

TABLE IV. — *Continued.*

PERTURBATIONS OF THE CO-ORDINATES IN UNITS OF THE SIXTH DECIMAL.
ARGUMENT I.

Arg.	ξ'	Diff.	η'	Diff.	ζ'	Diff.	Arg.	ξ'	Diff.	η'	Diff.	ζ'	Diff.
270°	+4588		-139		-291		315°	-644		-4428		-12	
271	4585	-3	294	-155	290	+1	316	825	-161	4392	+36	-5	+7
272	4576	9	450	156	289	1	317	1005	180	4347	45	+3	8
273	4561	15	606	156	287	2	316	1184	179	4296	51	9	6
274	4541	20	763	157	285	2	319	1361	177	4236	60	16	7
275	4515	26	910	156	283	2	320	1535	174	4170	66	22	6
276	4483	32	1076	167	281	2	321	1707	172	4096	74	28	6
277	4446	37	1231	155	278	3	322	1876	169	4015·	81	34	6
278	4402	44	1386	155	274	4	323	2042	166	3928	87	39	5
279	4353	49	1540	154	270	4	324	2205	163	3833	63	45	6
		56		163		4			159		102		5
280	+4297		-1693		-266		325	-2364		-3731		+50	
281	4236	-61	1844	-151	262	+4	326	2519	-155	3623	+108	54	+4
282	4169	67	1993	149	257	5	327	2670	151	3508	115	59	5
283	4095	74	2141	148	252	5	328	2817	147	3387	121	63	4
284	4016	79	2287	146	247	5	329	2958	141	3260	127	66	3
285	3931	85	2430	143	241	6	330	3095	137	3127	133	70	4
286	3840	91	2570	140	236	5	331	3226	131	2987	140	73	3
287	3744	96	2707	137	229	7	332	3352	126	2843	144	76	3
288	3641	103	2842	135	223	6	333	3472	120	2693	150	78	2
289	3533	108	2972	130	216	7	334	3586	114	2538	155	80	2
		113		127		6			107		166		2
290	+3420		-3099		-210		335	-3693		-2378		+82	
291	3301	-119	3222	-123	203	+7	336	3795	-102	2213	+165	83	+1
292	3177	124	3340	118	195	8	337	3890	95	2044	169	84	1
293	3047	130	3454	114	188	7	338	3977	87	1870	174	85	+1
294	2913	134	3563	109	180	8	339	4058	81	1693	177	85	0
295	2774	139	3667	104	173	7	340	4132	74	1512	181	85	0
296	2631	143	3766	99	165	8	341	4198	66	1328	194	85	0
297	2483	148	3860	94	157	8	342	4257	69	1140	188	84	-1
298	2331	152	3968	88	149	8	343	4308	51	950	190	83	1
299	2175	156	4030	82	141	8	344	4351	43	758	192	82	1
		160		76		9			36		195		2
300	+2015		-4106		-132		345	-4387		-563		+80	
301	1852	-163	4176	-70	124	+8	346	4414	-27	367	+196	78	-2
302	1686	166	4239	63	116	9	347	4434	20	-170	197	75	3
303	1516	170	4297	58	107	9	348	4445	11	+29	199	73	2
304	1344	172	4347	50	99	8	349	4448	-3	229	200	70	3
305	1169	175	4390	43	91	8	350	4442	+6	429	200	66	4
306	992	177	4427	37	82	9	351	4428	14	629	200	63	4
307	814	178	4456	29	74	8	352	4406	22	829	200	59	4
308	634	180	4479	23	66	8	353	4376	30	1028	199	54	5
309	453	181	4494	15	58	8	354	4337	39	1226	198	50	4
		182		7		8			47		197		5
310	+271		-4501		-50		355	-4290		+1423		+45	
311	+88	-183	4502	-1	42	+8	356	4234	+56	1619	+196	40	-5
312	-95	183	4494	+8	34	8	357	4170	64	1812	193	35	5
313	278	183	4480	14	26	8	358	4098	73	2003	191	29	6
314	461	183	4458	22	19	7	359	4018	80	2194	186	23	6
315	-644	183	-4428	+30	-12	+7	360	-3930	+88	+2377	+183	+17	-6

TABLE IV. — *Continued.*

PERTURBATIONS OF THE CO-ORDINATES IN UNITS OF THE SIXTH DECIMAL.
ARGUMENT II.

Arg.	ξ'	Diff.	η'	Diff.	ζ'	Diff.
0	+3377	−111	+2565	+126	− 4	+5
1	3266	115	2601	122	+ 1	6
2	3151	120	2913	117	7	5
3	3031	125	2930	112	12	6
4	2906	130	3042	106	18	6
5	2776	134	3148	100	24	6
6	2642	127	3248	95	30	7
7	2505	142	3343	90	37	6
8	2363	145	3433	84	43	6
9	2218	147	3517	77	49	7
10	+2069	−151	+3594	+71	+ 56	+7
11	1918	154	3665	65	63	7
12	1764	157	3730	59	70	7
13	1607	159	3789	53	77	7
14	1448	161	3842	46	84	7
15	1287	162	3888	39	91	7
16	1125	164	3927	32	98	7
17	961	165	3959	26	105	7
18	796	166	3985	19	112	7
19	630	166	4004	13	119	7
20	+ 464	−166	+4017	+ 7	+126	+7
21	298	167	4024	− 1	133	7
22	+ 131	166	4023	7	140	7
23	− 35	165	4016	14	147	7
24	200	164	4002	20	154	6
25	364	163	3982	27	160	7
26	527	162	3955	33	167	6
27	689	160	3922	40	173	6
28	849	158	3882	45	179	6
29	1007	155	3837	52	185	6
30	−1162	−153	+3785	− 58	+191	+5
31	1315	150	3727	63	196	6
32	1465	147	3664	69	202	5
33	1612	143	3595	75	207	5
34	1755	140	3520	80	212	5
35	1895	136	3440	85	217	4
36	2031	132	3355	90	221	4
37	2163	128	3265	95	225	4
38	2291	123	3170	99	229	4
39	2414	119	3071	104	233	5
40	−2533	−113	+2967	−108	+236	+3
41	2646	109	2859	112	239	2
42	2755	104	2747	116	241	3
43	2859	98	2631	119	244	2
44	2957	92	2512	123	246	1
45	−3049		+2389		+247	

Arg.	ξ'	Diff.	η'	Diff.	ζ'	Diff.
45	−3049	− 87	+2389	−126	+247	+1
46	3136	82	2263	128	246	1
47	3218	76	2135	131	249	1
48	3293	70	2004	133	250	+1
49	3363	63	1871	136	250	0
50	3426	58	1735	137	250	0
51	3484	51	1598	138	250	0
52	3535	46	1460	140	249	− 1
53	3586	33	1320	140	248	1
54	3619	33	1180	142	246	2
55	−3652	− 27	+1038	−141	+244	−2
56	3679	20	897	142	242	3
57	3699	16	755	142	239	3
58	3714	8	613	142	236	3
59	3722	− 2	472	141	233	3
60	3721	+ 4	331	141	230	3
61	3720	10	191	140	226	4
62	3710	16	+ 52	139	222	4
63	3694	21	− 85	137	217	5
64	3673	27	221	136	212	5
65	−3646	+ 33	− 356	−133	+207	− 6
66	3613	38	488	132	201	6
67	3575	43	618	130	196	6
68	3532	48	745	127	190	6
69	3484	54	869	124	183	7
70	3430	58	991	122	177	6
71	3372	63	1110	119	170	7
72	3309	67	1225	115	163	7
73	3242	71	1337	112	156	7
74	3171	70	1446	109	148	8
75	−3095	+ 79	−1551	−108	+141	−8
76	3016	83	1652	101	133	8
77	2933	86	1748	96	125	8
78	2847	90	1841	93	117	8
79	2757	92	1930	89	109	8
80	2665	95	2014	84	100	9
81	2570	98	2094	80	92	8
82	2472	101	2170	76	83	9
83	2371	102	2241	71	74	9
84	2269	104	2307	66	66	8
85	−2163	+106	−2369	− 57	+ 57	−9
86	2056	107	2426	53	48	9
87	1952	109	2479	47	39	9
88	1843	109	2526	44	30	9
89	1734	111	2570	38	21	9
90	−1623		−2608		+ 12	

TABLE IV. — *Continued.*

PERTURBATIONS OF THE CO-ORDINATES IN UNITS OF THE SIXTH DECIMAL.
ARGUMENT II.

Ang.	ξ'	Diff.	η'	Diff.	ζ'	Diff.	Arg.	ξ'	Diff.	η'	Diff.	ζ'	Diff.
90	−1623	+110	−2608	−34	+ 12	−9	135	+1744	+21	−1214	+53	−243	−1
91	1513	111	2642	30	+ 3	8	136	1765	21	1161	53	244	1
92	1402	111	2672	25	− 6	8	137	1785	20	1109	52	245	1
93	1290	112	2697	20	15	9	138	1803	18	1057	52	247	2
94	1179	111	2717	16	24	8	139	1820	17	1006	51	248	1
95	1068	111	2733	12	32	8	140	1835	15	957	49	248	0
96	958	110	2745	8	41	9	141	1849	14	907	50	249	1
97	848	110	2753	−3	49	8	142	1861	12	850	48	250	1
98	739	109	2756	+1	58	8	143	1873	12	812	47	250	0
99	632	107	2755		66	8	144	1883	10	765	47	251	−1
		107		4		8			10		45		0
100	− 525	+105	−2751	+9	+ 74	−8	145	+1893	+ 8	− 719	+45	−251	0
101	420	104	2742	12	82	8	146	1901	8	674	44	251	0
102	316	102	2730	15	90	8	147	1909	8	630	44	251	0
103	214	100	2715	19	98	8	148	1916	7	586	44	251	0
104	114	98	2696	23	106	7	149	1922	6	544	42	251	0
105	− 16	96	2673	25	113	7	150	1928	6	501	43	251	0
106	+ 80	94	2648	29	120	7	151	1933	5	460	41	251	0
107	174	92	2619	31	127	7	152	1938	5	419	41	251	0
108	266	89	2588	34	134	7	153	1942	4	379	40	251	0
109	355	88	2554	37	141	7	154	1946	4	339	40	251	0
		84		37		8			4		40		0
110	+ 441	+ 84	−2517	+39	+147	−7	155	+1950	+ 3	− 299	+39	−251	+1
111	525	82	2478	41	154	7	156	1953	3	260	38	250	1
112	607	79	2437	41	160	6	157	1956	3	222	38	250	0
113	686	76	2394	43	166	6	158	1959	3	184	38	250	0
114	762	76	2349	45	171	5	159	1962	3	145	39	249	1
115	835	73	2302	47	177	6	160	1964	2	107	38	249	0
116	906	71	2253	49	182	5	161	1967	3	70	37	249	0
117	973	67	2203	50	187	5	162	1969	2	− 32	38	248	1
118	1038	65	2152	51	192	5	163	1971	2	+ 7	39	248	0
119	1100	62	2100	52	197	5	164	1973	2	45	38	248	0
		60		54		4			2		38		1
120	+1160	+ 56	−2046	+54	+201	−4	165	+1975	+ 1	+ 83	+39	−247	+0
121	1216	54	1992	54	205	4	166	1976	1	122	39	247	0
122	1270	54	1938	56	209	4	167	1977	1	161	39	246	1
123	1322	52	1882	56	213	4	168	1978	1	201	40	246	0
124	1370	48	1826	56	216	3	169	1979	+1	240	39	246	0
125	1416	46	1770	56	220	4	170	1979	0	281	41	245	1
126	1460	44	1714	56	223	3	171	1978	− 1	322	41	245	0
127	1501	41	1657	57	226	3	172	1978	0	363	41	244	1
128	1539	38	1601	56	229	3	173	1976	2	405	42	244	1
129	1575	36	1545	56	231	2	174	1974	2	448	43	243	1
		34		57		3			2		44		0
130	+1609	+ 31	−1488	+55	+234	−2	175	+1972	− 4	+ 492	+44	−243	+0
131	1640	29	1433	56	236	2	176	1968	4	536	44	243	0
132	1669	27	1377	55	238	2	177	1964	4	581	45	242	1
133	1696	25	1322	54	240	1	178	1959	5	627	46	242	1
134	1721	23	1268	54	241	2	179	1953	6	674	47	241	1
135	+1744		−1214	54	+243	−2	180	+1946	− 7	+ 722	+48	−240	+1

TABLE IV. — *Continued.*

PERTURBATIONS OF THE CO-ORDINATES IN UNITS OF THE SIXTH DECIMAL.

ARGUMENT II.

Arg.	ξ'	Diff.	η'	Diff.	ζ'	Diff.	Arg.	ξ'	Diff.	η'	Diff.	ζ'	Diff.
180	+1946		+722		−240		225	−502		+2765		−83	
181	1938	−8	771	+49	240	0	226	607	−105	2760	+4	75	+8
182	1929	9	820	49	239	+1	227	714	107	2770	+1	67	8
183	1918	11	870	50	238	1	228	821	107	2766	−4	60	7
184	1905	13	921	51	237	1	229	929	108	2759	7	52	6
185	1892	13	973	52	236	1	230	1037	108	2748	11	44	8
186	1877	16	1025	52	235	1	231	1146	109	2732	16	36	8
187	1860	17	1079	54	234	1	232	1255	109	2713	19	27	9
188	1841	19	1133	54	233	1	233	1364	109	2689	24	19	8
189	1821	20	1187	54	232	1	234	1473	109	2661	28	11	8
190	+1799	22	+1242	55	−231	1	235	−1582	109	+2620	32	−2	9
191	1775	24	1298	56	229	+2	236	1690	−108	2593	−26	+7	+6
192	1748	26	1354	56	226	1	237	1798	108	2552	41	15	8
193	1720	29	1411	57	224	2	238	1905	107	2507	45	24	9
194	1689	31	1468	57	222	2	239	2010	105	2457	50	32	9
195	1656	33	1525	57	220	2	240	2115	106	2403	54	41	8
196	1621	35	1582	57	218	2	241	2218	103	2345	58	50	9
197	1583	38	1639	57	216	2	242	2320	102	2282	63	58	8
198	1543	40	1696	57	214	2	243	2420	100	2215	67	67	9
199	1500	43	1753	57	213	3	244	2518	98	2144	71	75	8
200	+1455	45	+1810	57	−210	3	245	−2613	95	+2060	75	+84	9
201	1407	−48	1867	56	208	+2	246	2706	−93	1989	−80	92	+8
202	1357	50	1923	56	205	3	247	2796	90	1906	83	101	9
203	1304	53	1978	55	201	4	248	2883	87	1818	86	109	8
204	1248	56	2032	54	198	3	249	2967	84	1726	92	117	8
205	1190	58	2086	54	194	4	250	3047	80	1631	95	125	8
206	1129	61	2139	53	191	3	251	3124	77	1532	99	133	8
207	1065	64	2190	51	187	4	252	3198	74	1429	103	140	7
208	998	67	2240	50	183	4	253	3267	69	1322	107	148	8
209	920	69	2289	49	178	5	254	3333	66	1213	109	155	7
210	+857	72	+2336	47	−174	4	255	−3394	61	+1100	113	+162	7
211	782	−76	2382	+46	169	+5	256	3452	−58	984	−110	169	+7
212	705	77	2426	44	164	5	257	3504	52	865	119	176	7
213	626	79	2468	42	159	5	258	3552	48	743	122	183	7
214	544	82	2507	39	154	6	259	3595	43	618	125	189	6
215	450	85	2545	38	148	6	260	3633	38	491	127	195	6
216	372	87	2580	35	142	6	261	3665	32	362	129	200	5
217	283	89	2612	32	136	6	262	3693	28	231	131	206	6
218	191	92	2642	30	130	6	263	3715	22	+98	133	211	5
219	98	93	2669	27	124	6	264	3732	17	−37	135	216	6
220	+2	96	+2693	24	−117	7	265	−3743	11	−173	136	+221	6
221	−95	−97	2714	+21	111	+6	266	3748	−5	310	−137	225	+4
222	195	100	2732	18	104	7	267	3748	0	448	138	229	4
223	296	101	2746	14	97	7	268	3742	+6	587	139	233	4
224	398	102	2757	11	90	7	269	3730	12	726	139	236	3
225	−502	−104	−2765	+6	−83	+7	270	−3712	+19	−866	−140	+239	+3

TABLE IV. — *Continued.*

PERTURBATIONS OF THE CO-ORDINATES IN UNITS OF THE SIXTH DECIMAL.

ARGUMENT II.

Arg.	ξ'	Diff.	η'	Diff.	ζ'	Diff.	Arg.	ξ'	Diff.	η'	Diff.	ζ'	Diff.
270	−3712	+21	−866	−140	+239	+3	315	+1820	+154	−3753	+68	+71	−7
271	3688	30	1006	139	242	2	316	1974	152	3685	74	64	7
272	3658	36	1145	89	244	2	317	2126	148	3611	80	57	7
273	3622	42	1234	189	246	2	318	2274	146	3531	86	51	6
274	3580	48	1423	137	247	1	319	2419	141	3445	92	44	7
275	3532	54	1560	136	249	2	320	2560	137	3353	97	38	6
276	3478	59	1696	135	250	+1	321	2697	133	3256	104	31	7
277	3419	66	1831	133	250	0	322	2830	129	3152	109	25	6
278	3353	72	1964	131	250	0	323	2959	124	3043	114	19	6
279	3281	77	2095	129	250	0	324	3083	119	2929	119	13	6
280	−3204	+83	−2224	−126	+250	0	325	+3202	+114	−2810	+124	+8	−6
281	3121	89	2350	123	249	−1	326	3316	109	2686	128	+2	6
282	3032	95	2473	121	247	2	327	3425	103	2558	133	−3	5
283	2937	99	2594	117	246	1	328	3523	102	2425	137	8	5
284	2838	105	2711	114	244	2	329	3625	92	2288	142	13	4
285	2733	111	2825	110	242	2	330	3717	86	2146	146	17	4
286	2622	115	2935	107	239	3	331	3803	79	2001	148	21	4
287	2507	120	3042	102	237	2	332	3882	73	1853	152	25	4
288	2387	124	3144	97	234	3	333	3955	67	1701	154	29	3
289	2263	129	3241	93	230	4	334	4022	60	1547	157	32	3
290	−2134	+133	−3334	−89	+226	−4	335	+4082	+54	−1390	+160	−35	−2
291	2001	138	3423	84	222	4	336	4136	47	1230	162	37	3
292	1863	141	3507	78	218	4	337	4183	40	1068	163	40	2
293	1722	144	3585	73	213	5	338	4223	33	905	165	42	1
294	1578	148	3658	67	208	5	339	4256	26	740	167	43	2
295	1430	152	3725	62	203	5	340	4282	19	573	167	45	1
296	1278	154	3787	56	198	5	341	4301	12	406	168	46	−1
297	1124	161	3843	50	192	6	342	4313	+5	238	168	47	0
298	963	163	3893	43	187	5	343	4318	−2	−70	168	47	0
299	800	154	3936	38	181	6	344	4316	−8	+98	169	47	0
300	−646	+161	−3974	−31	+175	−7	345	+4308	−16	+267	+167	−47	+1
301	485	164	4005	25	168	6	346	4292	23	434	167	46	1
302	321	166	4030	19	162	7	347	4269	30	601	166	45	1
303	−155	167	4049	12	155	7	348	4230	38	767	164	44	2
304	+12	167	4061	−6	148	7	349	4203	43	931	162	42	2
305	179	167	4066	+1	141	6	350	4160	50	1093	161	40	2
306	346	168	4065	8	135	7	351	4110	57	1254	158	38	2
307	514	167	4057	15	128	7	352	4053	63	1412	156	35	3
308	681	167	4042	21	121	7	353	3990	69	1568	153	32	3
309	848	166	4021	28	114	8	354	3921	76	1721	150	29	4
310	+1014	+165	−3993	+35	+106	−7	355	+3845	−82	+1871	+146	−25	+3
311	1179	163	3958	42	99	7	356	3763	88	2017	143	22	4
312	1342	161	3916	46	92	7	357	3675	94	2160	139	18	5
313	1503	159	3868	48	85	7	358	3581	99	2299	135	13	4
314	1662	158	3814	54	78	7	359	3482	−106	2434	131	9	4
315	+1820		−3753		+71		360	+3377		+2565		−4	

38

TABLE IV. — *Continued.*

PERTURBATIONS OF THE CO-ORDINATES IN UNITS OF THE SIXTH DECIMAL.
ARGUMENT III.

Arg.	ξ'	Diff.	η'	Diff.	ζ'	Diff.	Arg.	ξ'	Diff.	η'	Diff.	ζ'	Diff.
0	-2415	+19	+1351	+39	-186		45	-901	+49	+2619	+13	-95	
1	2396	20	1390	38		+3	46	852	49	2634	15		+10
2	2376	21	1429	38			47	803	49	2649	15		
3	2355	21	1466	38	183		48	754	50	2663	14	85	
4	2334	21	1504	38			49	704	51	2677	14		
5	2312	22	1541	37		4	50	653	51	2690	13		10
6	2290	22	1578	37	179		51	602	52	2702	12	75	
7	2267	23	1615	37			52	550	52	2714	12		
8	2243	24	1651	36		3	53	498	52	2725	11		12
9	2219	24	1686	35	176		54	446	52	2735	10	63	
		25		35					52		10		
10	-2194	+20	+1721	+35		4	55	-394	+53	+2745	+9		12
11	2169	26	1756	34			56	341	53	2754	8		
12	2142	26	1790	34	172		57	288	53	2762	8	51	
13	2115	27	1824	34			58	234	54	2770	8		
14	2088	27	1857	33		5	59	180	54	2777	7		12
15	2060	28	1890	33	167		60	126	54	2783	6	39	
16	2031	29	1922	32			61	72	54	2788	6		
17	2002	29	1954	32		5	62	-18	54	2793	5		12
18	1972	30	1985	31	162		63	+37	56	2796	3	27	
19	1941	31	2016	31			64	92	55	2799	3		
		31		30		5			55		3		13
20	-1910	+32	+2046	+29			65	+147	+55	+2802	+1		
21	1878	33	2075	29	157		66	202	55	2803	1	-14	
22	1845	33	2104	29			67	257	55	2803	0		
23	1811	34	2133	28		6	68	312	55	2803	0		14
24	1777	34	2161	28	151		69	367	55	2802	-1	0	
25	1742	35	2188	27			70	422	55	2800	2		
26	1706	36	2215	27		7	71	477	55	2797	3		14
27	1670	36	2241	26	144		72	532	55	2793	4	+14	
28	1633	37	2267	26			73	587	55	2789	4		
29	1595	38	2292	26		7	74	642	55	2783	5		14
		38		25					55		7		
30	-1557	+39	+2317	+24	137		75	+697	+54	+2776	-7	28	
31	1518	39	2341	24			76	751	55	2769	9		
32	1478	40	2364	23		7	77	806	55	2760	9		14
33	1437	41	2387	23	130		78	860	54	2751	9	42	
34	1396	41	2410	23			79	914	54	2740	11		
35	1354	42	2432	22		8	80	967	53	2728	12		14
36	1312	42	2453	21	122		81	1020	53	2716	12	56	
37	1269	43	2474	21			82	1073	53	2702	14		
38	1225	44	2494	20		8	83	1126	53	2687	15		15
39	1180	45	2514	20	114		84	1179	53	2672	15	71	
		45		19					52		17		
40	-1135	+46	+2533	+18		9	85	+1231	+51	+2655	-18		14
41	1089	46	2551	18			86	1282	51	2637	18		
42	1043	47	2569	18	105		87	1333	51	2618	19	85	
43	996	47	2586	17			88	1384	51	2598	20		
44	949	+48	2603	17		+10	89	1434	50	2577	21		+14
45	-901		+2619	+16	-95		90	+1484	+50	+2554	-23	+99	

TABLE IV. — *Continued.*

PERTURBATIONS OF THE CO-ORDINATES IN UNITS OF THE SIXTH DECIMAL.
ARGUMENT III.

Arg.	ξ'	Diff.	η'	Diff.	ζ'	Diff.	Arg.	ξ'	Diff.	η'	Diff.	ζ'	Diff.
90	+1484	+50	+2554	−23	+ 99		135	+3026	+14	+ 599	−56	+243	
91	1534	49	2531	25		+14	136	3040	13	543	56		+2
92	1583	48	2506	25			137	3053	12	487	56		
93	1631	48	2481	27	113		138	3065	11	431	56	245	
94	1679	47	2454	28		14	139	3076	10	375	55		+2
95	1726	47	2426	28			140	3086	9	320	56		
96	1773	46	2398	30	127		141	3095	8	264	56	247	
97	1819	46	2368	32		13	142	3103	6	208	55		0
98	1865	45	2336	32			143	3109	6	153	56		
99	1910	44	2304	33	140		144	3115	4	97	55	247	
100	+1954	+44	+2271	−34		13	145	+3119	+3	+ 42	−55		−1
101	1998	43	2237	35			146	3122	2	− 13	54		
102	2041	42	2202	37	153		147	3124	+1	67	55	246	
103	2083	42	2165	37		13	148	3125	0	122	54		2
104	2125	41	2128	38			149	3125	−2	176	54		
105	2166	41	2090	40	166		150	3123	2	230	53	244	
106	2207	39	2050	40		12	151	3121	4	283	53		3
107	2246	39	2010	41			152	3117	5	336	53		
108	2285	39	1969	42	178		153	3112	6	389	52	241	
109	2324	37	1927	43		11	154	3106	8	441	52		3
110	+2361	+37	+1884	−44			155	+3098	−8	− 493	−52		
111	2398	36	1840	45	189		156	3090	10	545	51	238	
112	2434	35	1795	46		10	157	3080	11	596	50		5
113	2469	35	1749	46			158	3069	13	646	50		
114	2504	34	1703	47	199		159	3056	13	696	50	233	
115	2538	32	1656	48		9	160	3043	15	746	49		5
116	2570	32	1608	49			161	3028	15	795	49		
117	2602	32	1559	49	208		162	3013	17	844	48	228	
118	2634	30	1510	50		8	163	2996	18	892	48		6
119	2664	30	1460	51			164	2978	19	940	47		
120	+2694	+28	+1409	−51	216		165	+2959	−21	− 987	−47	222	
121	2722	28	1358	52		8	166	2938	21	1034	46		6
122	2750	27	1306	52			167	2917	23	1080	46		
123	2777	26	1254	52	224		168	2894	24	1126	45	216	
124	2803	25	1201	53		8	169	2870	25	1171	44		7
125	2828	24	1148	53			170	2845	26	1215	44		
126	2852	24	1094	54	230		171	2819	27	1259	44	209	
127	2875	23	1040	54		6	172	2792	28	1303	44		8
128	2898	23	986	54			173	2764	29	1346	43		
129	2919	21	931	55	236		174	2735	30	1388	42	201	
130	+2939	+20	+ 876	−55		4	175	+2705	−31	−1429	−42		8
131	2959	18	821	55			176	2674	32	1471	41		
132	2977	17	766	55	240		177	2642	33	1512	41	193	
133	2994	17	711	56		+ 3	178	2609	34	1552	40		−8
134	3011	15	655	56			179	2575	35	1591	39		
135	+3026		+ 599	−56	+243		180	+2540		−1630	−39	+185	

TABLE IV. — *Continued.*

PERTURBATIONS OF THE CO-ORDINATES IN UNITS OF THE SIXTH DECIMAL.

ARGUMENT III.

Arg.	ξ'	Diff.	η'	Diff.	ζ'	Diff.	Arg.	ξ'	Diff.	η'	Diff.	ζ'	Diff.
180°	+2540		−1630		+185		225°	+ 463		−2740		+ 42	
181	2504	−36	1660	−39			226	414	−49	2747	− 7		
182	2467	37	1707	38		− 9	227	365	49	2754	7		− 9
183	2430	37	1744	37	176		228	317	48	2759	5	33	
184	2392	38	1781	37			229	269	48	2764	5		
185	2353	39	1817	36		0	230	221	48	2769	4		10
186	2313	40	1853	36	167		231	173	48	2771	3	23	
187	2272	41	1888	35			232	125	48	2773	2		
188	2231	41	1922	34		9	233	78	47	2774	− 1		10
189	2189	42	1956	34	158		234	+ 30	46	2774	0	13	
		43		33					47		+ 1		
190	+2146		−1989			0	235	− 17		−2773			10
191	2103	−43	2022	−33			236	64	−47	2771	+ 2		
192	2059	44	2054	32	149		237	111	47	2768	2	+ 3	
193	2015	44	2086	32			238	157	46	2765	3		
194	1970	45	2117	31		10	239	203	46	2760	5		10
195	1925	45	2147	30	139		240	249	46	2754	6	− 7	
196	1879	46	2177	30			241	295	46	2748	6		
197	1833	46	2206	29		9	242	341	46	2740	8		10
198	1786	47	2235	29	130		243	387	46	2732	8	17	
199	1739	47	2263	28			244	432	45	2723	9		
		47		27					45		10		
200	+1692		−2290			10	245	− 477		−2713			10
201	1644	−48	2317	−27	120		246	522	−45	2702	+11	27	
202	1596	48	2343	26			247	566	44	2690	12		
203	1549	48	2369	26		9	248	611	45	2677	13		9
204	1499	49	2393	24	111		249	655	44	2663	11	36	
205	1450	49	2417	24			250	699	44	2649	14		
206	1401	49	2441	24		10	251	742	43	2634	16		10
207	1352	49	2463	22	101		252	786	44	2617	17	46	
208	1303	49	2485	22			253	829	43	2600	17		
209	1254	49	2506	21		10	254	872	43	2582	18		9
		50		21					43		18		
210	+1204		−2527		91		255	− 915		−2563		55	
211	1175	−49	2547	−20			256	957	−42	2544	+19		
212	1105	51	2566	19		10	257	1000	43	2523	21		10
213	1055	50	2584	18	81		258	1042	42	2502	21	65	
214	1006	49	2602	18			259	1083	41	2481	21		
215	956	50	2618	16		9	260	1125	42	2458	23		9
216	906	50	2634	16	72		261	1166	41	2435	23	74	
217	857	49	2649	15			262	1207	41	2411	24		
218	807	50	2663	14		10	263	1248	41	2387	24		9
219	758	49	2677	14	62		264	1288	40	2362	25	83	
		50		13					40		26		
220	+ 708		−2690			10	265	−1328		−2336			9
221	659	−49	2701	−11			266	1368	−40	2310	+26		
222	610	49	2712	11	52		267	1407	39	2283	27	92	
223	561	49	2722	10			268	1446	39	2255	28		
224	512	49	2732	10		−10	269	1485	39	2227	28		− 8
225	+ 463	−49	−2740	− 8	+ 42		270	−1523	−38	−2198	+29	−100	

TABLE IV. — *Continued.*

PERTURBATIONS OF THE CO-ORDINATES IN UNITS OF THE SIXTH DECIMAL.
ARGUMENT III.

Arg.	ξ'	Diff.	η'	Diff.	ζ	Diff.	Arg.	ξ'	Diff.	η'	Diff.	ζ	Diff.
270	-1523	-38	-2198	+29	-100		315	-2673	-9	-554	+41	-188	
271	1561	38	2169	30		-9	316	2682	8	513	42		-3
272	1599	37	2139	30			317	2690	8	471	42		
273	1636	37	2109	30	109		318	2698	8	429	42	191	
274	1673	37	2079	30		8	319	2705	7	387	42		2
275	1710	37	2048	31			320	2711	6	345	42		
276	1746	36	2016	32	117		321	2716	5	303	42	193	
277	1781	35	1984	32		8	322	2720	4	260	43		1
278	1816	35	1951	33			323	2724	4	217	43		
279	1851	35	1918	33	125		324	2728	4	175	42	194	
		34		33					2		43		
280	-1885	-33	-1885	+33		7	325	-2730	-2	-132	+43		2
281	1918	33	1852	34			326	2732	-2	89	43		
282	1951	33	1818	34	132		327	2733	-1	46	43	196	
283	1984	33	1784	34			328	2733	0	-3	43		
284	2016	31	1749	35		7	329	2733	0	+40	43		-1
285	2047	31	1714	35	139		330	2732	+1	84	44	197	
286	2078	31	1679	35			331	2730	2	127	43		
287	2109	31	1643	36		7	332	2727	3	170	43		0
288	2138	29	1607	36	146		333	2724	3	214	44	197	
289	2167	29	1571	36			334	2720	4	257	43		
		29		36		8			4		43		0
290	-2196	-27	-1535	+37			335	-2716	+5	+300	+44		0
291	2223	27	1498	37	152		336	2711	6	344	44	197	
292	2250	27	1461	37			337	2705	6	387	43		
293	2277	26	1424	37		6	338	2699	6	431	44		0
294	2303	25	1387	37	158		339	2692	7	474	43	197	
295	2328	24	1349	38			340	2685	7	517	44		
296	2352	24	1311	38		6	341	2677	8	561	44		0
297	2376	24	1273	38	164		342	2668	9	604	43	197	
298	2399	23	1235	38			343	2659	9	647	43		
299	2421	22	1196	39		5	344	2649	10	690	43		+1
		22		38					10		43		
300	-2443	-20	-1158	+39	169		345	-2639	+11	+733	+42	196	
301	2463	20	1119	39			346	2628	11	775	43		
302	2483	20	1080	39		5	347	2616	12	818	43		2
303	2502	19	1040	40	174		348	2604	12	860	42	194	
304	2521	19	1001	39			349	2592	12	902	42		
305	2538	17	961	40		4	350	2579	13	944	42		1
306	2555	17	921	40	178		351	2565	14	986	42	193	
307	2571	16	881	40			352	2550	15	1028	42		
308	2587	16	841	40		4	353	2535	15	1069	41		2
309	2602	15	801	40	182		354	2520	15	1110	41	191	
		14		41					16		41		
310	-2616	-16	-760	+41		3	355	-2504	+17	+1151	+41		2
311	2630	13	719	41			356	2487	17	1192	41		
312	2641	12	679	41	185		357	2470	17	1232	40	189	
313	2652	11	637	41			358	2452	18	1272	40		
314	2663	11	596	41		-3	359	2434	18	1311	39		+3
315	-2673	-10	-554	+42	-128		360	-2415	+19	+1351	+40	-186	

TABLE IV. — *Continued.*

PERTURBATIONS OF THE CO-ORDINATES IN UNITS OF THE SIXTH DECIMAL. ARGUMENT IV.

Arg.	ξ'	Diff.	η'	Diff.	ζ'	Diff.	Arg.	ξ'	Diff.	η'	Diff.	ζ'	Diff.
0	−1682	+50	+2878	+28	+160		45	+822	+56	+3243	−14	−2	
1	1632	50	2906	28			46	878	56	3229	−15		
2	1582	51	2934	27		−9	47	934	56	3214	−16		−12
3	1531	51	2961	26	151		48	990	55	3198	−18	14	
4	1480	52	2987	25			49	1045	55	3180	−18		
5	1428	52	3012	25		9	50	1100	55	3162	−18		11
6	1376	52	3037	23	142		51	1155	55	3144	−20	25	
7	1324	53	3060	22			52	1210	54	3124	−21		
8	1271	53	3082	22		9	53	1264	54	3103	−22		12
9	1218	53	3104	21	133		54	1318	53	3081	−23	37	
10	−1164	54	+3125	19		10	55	+1371	+53	+3058	−23		12
11	1110	54	3144	19			56	1424	53	3035	−25		
12	1056	54	3163	18	123		57	1477	52	3010	−25	49	
13	1001	55	3181	17			58	1529	52	2985	−26		
14	946	55	3198	16		11	59	1581	52	2959	−27		11
15	891	55	3214	15	112		60	1633	51	2932	−28	60	
16	835	56	3229	14			61	1684	50	2904	−29		
17	779	56	3243	14		10	62	1734	50	2875	−30		12
18	723	56	3257	12	102		63	1784	49	2845	−31	72	
19	667	56	3269	11			64	1833	49	2814	−31		
20	−611	+57	+3280	10		11	65	+1882	+48	+2783	−33		11
21	554	57	3290	10	91		66	1930	48	2750	−33	83	
22	497	57	3300	8			67	1978	47	2717	−34		
23	440	57	3308	7		11	68	2025	47	2683	−35		11
24	383	57	3315	7	80		69	2072	46	2648	−35	94	
25	326	58	3322	5			70	2118	45	2613	−37		
26	268	57	3327	4		11	71	2163	45	2576	−37		11
27	211	58	3331	4	69		72	2208	44	2539	−38	105	
28	153	58	3335	2			73	2252	44	2501	−39		
29	95	57	3337	2		12	74	2296	42	2462	−39		10
30	−38	+58	+3339	0	57		75	+2338	+42	+2423	−41	115	
31	+20	58	3339	0			76	2380	42	2382	−41		
32	78	58	3339	−2		12	77	2422	41	2341	−42		10
33	136	57	3337	−2	45		78	2463	40	2299	−42	125	
34	193	58	3335	−4			79	2503	39	2257	−43		
35	251	58	3331	−4		11	80	2542	38	2214	−44		10
36	309	57	3327	−5	34		81	2580	38	2170	−45	135	
37	366	58	3322	−7			82	2618	37	2125	−45		
38	424	57	3315	−7		12	83	2655	36	2080	−46		9
39	481	57	3308	−9	22		84	2691	35	2034	−46	144	
40	+538	+57	+3299	−9		12	85	+2726	+35	+1988	−47		9
41	595	57	3290	−10			86	2761	34	1941	−48		
42	652	57	3280	−12	+10		87	2795	33	1893	−48	153	
43	709	57	3268	−12			88	2828	32	1845	−49		
44	766	56	3256	−13		−11	89	2860	41	1796	−49		−9
45	+822		+3243		−2		90	+2901	+31	+1747		162	

TABLE IV.— Continued.

PERTURBATIONS OF THE CO-ORDINATES IN UNITS OF THE SIXTH DECIMAL.
ARGUMENT IV.

Arg.	ξ'	Diff.	η'	Diff.	ζ'	Diff.	Arg.	ξ'	Diff.	η'	Diff.	ζ'	Diff.
90	+2891		+1747		-162		135	+3285		-808		-231	
91	2921	+30	1697	-50			136	3270	-15	866	-58		
92	2950	29	1646	51		-8	137	3254	16	924	58		0
93	2979	29	1595	51	170		138	3237	17	981	57	231	
94	3006	27	1544	61			139	3218	19	1038	57		
95	3033	27	1492	62		6	140	3199	19	1095	57		+1
96	3059	26	1439	53	178		141	3179	20	1151	56	230	
97	3084	25	1386	53			142	3158	21	1207	56		
98	3108	24	1332	54		7	143	3136	22	1263	56		1
99	3131	23	1278	54	185		144	3113	23	1319	56	229	
		27		61					24		55		
100	+3153		+1224			7	145	+3089		-1374			2
101	3174	+21	1169	-55			146	3064	-25	1428	-54		
102	3194	20	1114	55	192		147	3038	26	1483	55	227	
103	3213	19	1059	55			148	3011	27	1536	53		
104	3231	18	1003	56		6	149	2984	27	1590	54		3
105	3248	17	947	56	198		150	2955	29	1643	53	224	
106	3265	17	890	57			151	2925	30	1695	52		
107	3280	16	833	57		6	152	2894	31	1747	52		3
108	3294	14	776	57	204		153	2863	31	1798	51	221	
109	3307	13	719	57			154	2830	33	1849	51		
		12		58		6			33		50		4
110	+3319		+661				155	+2797		-1899			
111	3331	+12	604	-57	210		156	2763	-34	1949	-50	217	
112	3341	10	546	58			157	2728	35	1998	49		
113	3350	9	487	59		5	158	2692	36	2046	48		4
114	3358	8	429	58	215		159	2655	37	2094	48	213	
115	3365	7	370	59			160	2617	38	2141	47		
116	3371	6	312	59		4	161	2579	38	2188	47		5
117	3376	6	253	59	219		162	2539	40	2234	46	208	
118	3379	3	194	59			163	2499	40	2279	45		
119	3382	3	135	59		3	164	2458	41	2323	44		6
		2		60					41		44		
120	+3384		+75		222		165	+2417		-2367		202	
121	3385	+1	+16	-59			166	2374	-43	2410	-43		
122	3384	-1	-43	60		3	167	2331	43	2452	42		6
123	3383	1	102	59	225		168	2287	44	2494	42	196	
124	3381	2	162	60			169	2243	44	2534	40		
125	3377	4	221	59		3	170	2197	46	2574	40		7
126	3373	4	280	59	228		171	2151	46	2613	39	189	
127	3367	6	339	59			172	2105	46	2652	39		
128	3360	7	398	59		1	173	2057	48	2689	37		7
129	3353	7	457	59	229		174	2009	46	2726	37	182	
		9		59					48		36		
130	+3344		-516			1	175	+1961		-2762			8
131	3334	-10	575	-59			176	1911	-50	2797	-35		
132	3323	11	634	59	230		177	1861	50	2831	34	174	
133	3311	12	692	58			178	1811	50	2864	33		
134	3298	13	750	58		-1	179	1760	51	2897	33		+6
135	+3285	-13	-808	-56	-231		180	+1708	-52	-2929	-31	-166	

TABLE IV. — *Continued.*

PERTURBATIONS OF THE CO-ORDINATES IN UNITS OF THE SIXTH DECIMAL.
ARGUMENT IV.

Arg.	ξ'	Diff.	η'	Diff.	ζ'	Diff.	Arg.	ξ'	Diff.	η'	Diff.	ζ'	Diff.
180	+1708	−52	−2928	−30	−166		225	−867	−57	−3297		+1	
181	1656	62	2958	30		+9	226	944	57	3281	+16		+2
182	1614	63	2988	29			227	1001	66	3264	17		
183	1551	54	3017	27	157		228	1057	66	3246	18	13	
184	1497	54	3044	27		10	229	1113	66	3227	19		
185	1443	61	3071	27			230	1160	56	3207	20		12
186	1390	65	3097	26	147		231	1224	65	3186	21	25	
187	1334	66	3122	26			232	1279	55	3164	22		
188	1278	55	3146	24		9	233	1334	65	3141	23		13
189	1223	56	3169	23	138		234	1388	64	3117	24	38	
190	+1167	−57	−3190	21		10	235	−1442	−55	−3092	25		13
191	1110	57	3211	−21			236	1495	52	3066	+26		
192	1053	67	3231	20	128		237	1547	52	3039	27	50	
193	996	57	3250	19		11	238	1599	52	3011	28		
194	939	66	3268	18			239	1651	52	2983	28		12
195	881	58	3285	17	117		240	1702	51	2953	30	62	
196	823	68	3301	16			241	1752	50	2922	31		
197	765	58	3315	14		11	242	1802	50	2891	31		12
198	707	69	3329	14	106		243	1852	50	2859	32	74	
199	648	59	3342	13			244	1901	49	2826	33		
200	+589	−59	−3353	11		11	245	−1949	−47	−2792	34		11
201	530	59	3364	−11	95		246	1996	47	2757	+35	85	
202	471	59	3373	9			247	2043	47	2721	36		
203	412	60	3382	9		11	248	2090	45	2684	37		12
204	352	59	3389	7	84		249	2135	45	2647	37	97	
205	293	60	3395	6			250	2180	44	2609	38		
206	233	59	3401	6		12	251	2224	44	2570	39		11
207	174	60	3405	4	72		252	2268	43	2530	40	108	
208	114	60	3408	3			253	2311	42	2489	41		
209	+54	59	3410	2		11	254	2353	41	2448	41		11
210	−5	−60	−3411	−1	61		255	−2394	−40	−2406	42		11
211	65	60	3410	+1			256	2434	40	2363	+43	119	
212	125	59	3409	1		12	257	2474	39	2310	44		
213	184	60	3407	2	49		258	2513	38	2275	44		10
214	244	60	3404	3			259	2551	39	2230	45	129	
215	303	69	3399	5		13	260	2589	39	2185	45		
216	362	69	3394	5	36		261	2626	37	2139	46		10
217	421	66	3387	7			262	2661	36	2092	47	139	
218	480	59	3380	7		12	263	2696	35	2044	48		
219	539	59	3371	9	24		264	2730	34	1996	48	149	
220	−598	−56	−3361	10		12	265	−2764	−32	−1948	49		10
221	656	58	3350	+11			266	2796	33	1899	+49	158	
222	714	66	3339	11	−12		267	2828	30	1849	50		
223	772	68	3326	13		+13	268	2858	30	1799	50		+9
224	830	−57	3312	14			269	2888	30	1748	51		
225	−887		−3297	+15	+1		270	−2917	−29	−1696	+52	+167	

TABLE IV.— Continued.

PERTURBATIONS OF THE CO-ORDINATES IN UNITS OF THE SIXTH DECIMAL.
ARGUMENT IV.

Arg.	ξ'	Diff.	η'	Diff.	ζ'	Diff.	Arg.	ξ'	Diff.	η'	Diff.	ζ'	Diff.
270	-2917	-28	-1696	+52	+167		315	-3220	+16	+808	+66	+232	
271	2945	27	1644	52			316	3204	17	918	66		
272	2972	26	1592	53	+8		317	3187	16	974	56		0
273	2998	26	1539	53	175		318	3169	19	1030	55	232	
274	3024	24	1486	53			319	3150	19	1085	54		
275	3048	23	1433	54	8		320	3131	21	1139	55		-2
276	3071	23	1379	55	183		321	3110	21	1194	54	230	
277	3094	21	1324	55			322	3089	23	1248	53		
278	3115	21	1269	55	8		323	3066	23	1301	53		2
279	3136	19	1214	56	191		324	3043	24	1354	53	228	
280	-3155	-19	-1158	+56	7		325	-3019	+25	+1407	+52	2	
281	3174	18	1102	56			326	2994	26	1459	52		
282	3192	16	1046	56	198		327	2968	27	1511	52	226	
283	3208	16	990	57			328	2941	27	1563	52		
284	3224	15	933	57	6		329	2914	29	1614	51	3	
285	3239	14	876	57	204		330	2885	29	1664	50	223	
286	3253	12	819	57			331	2856	30	1714	50		
287	3265	12	762	58	5		332	2826	31	1763	49	4	
288	3277	11	704	58	209		333	2795	32	1812	49	219	
289	3288	10	646	58			334	2763	33	1860	48		
290	-3298	-9	-588	+58	5		335	-2730	+33	+1908	+47	5	
291	3307	9	530	58	214		336	2697	34	1955	46	214	
292	3314	7	472	58			337	2663	35	2001	46		
293	3321	7	414	58	5		338	2628	36	2047	45	5	
294	3327	6	355	59	219		339	2592	37	2092	45	209	
295	3332	5	297	59			340	2555	37	2137	44		
296	3336	4	238	59	4		341	2518	38	2181	43	5	
297	3338	2	179	59	223		342	2480	39	2224	43	204	
298	3340	2	121	58			343	2441	39	2267	42		
299	3341	-1	62	59	3		344	2402	41	2309	41	0	
300	-3341	0	-4	+59	226		345	-2361	+41	+2350	+40	198	
301	3340	+1	+55	59			346	2320	41	2390	40		
302	3338	2	114	59	2		347	2279	42	2430	40	7	
303	3334	4	172	58	228		348	2237	43	2469	39	191	
304	3330	4	231	59			349	2194	44	2508	39		
305	3325	5	289	58	2		350	2150	44	2545	37	7	
306	3319	6	347	58	230		351	2106	45	2582	37	184	
307	3312	7	405	58			352	2061	45	2618	36		
308	3304	8	463	58	+2		353	2016	46	2654	36	7	
309	3295	9	521	58	232		354	1970	47	2698	34	177	
310	-3284	11	+578	+57	0		355	-1923	+47	+2722	+33	8	
311	3273	+11	635	57			356	1876	48	2755	33		
312	3261	12	692	57	232		357	1828	48	2787	32	169	
313	3248	13	749	57			358	1780	49	2818	31		
314	3234	14	806	57	0		359	1731	49	2848	30	-9	
315	-3220	+14	+862	+56	+232		360	-1682	+49	+2878	+30	+160	

TABLE IV. — *Continued.*

PERTURBATIONS OF THE CO-ORDINATES IN UNITS OF THE SIXTH DECIMAL.
ARGUMENT V.

Arg.	ξ'	Diff.	η'	Diff.	ζ'	Diff.	Arg.	ξ'	Diff.	η'	Diff.	ζ'	Diff.
0	+1204	—14	+ 758	+21	—2		45	+304	—25	+1374	+ 5	—1	
1	1190	14	779	20			46	279	24	1379	5		
2	1176	16	799	20			47	255	24	1384	5		
3	1161	14	819	20	2		48	230	26	1389	4	1	
4	1147	16	839	20			49	206	24	1392	4		
5	1132	16	859	20			50	181	26	1395	2		
6	1116	16	878	19	2		51	156	25	1398	3	1	
7	1100	16	897	19			52	131	25	1401	3		
8	1084	16	916	18			53	106	25	1403	2		
9	1068	17	934	18	2		54	81	25	1404	1	1	
10	+1051	—17	+ 952	18			55	+ 56	—25	+1405	+ 1		
11	1034	17	970	18			56	31	20	1406	+ 1		
12	1017	17	988	18	2		57	+ 6	25	1407	0	1	
13	999	18	1005	17			58	— 19	25	1407	—1		
14	981	18	1022	17			59	44	25	1406	1		
15	963	18	1039	17	2		60	69	25	1405	1	1	
16	944	19	1056	17			61	94	26	1404	2		
17	925	19	1072	16			62	119	20	1402	2		
18	906	19	1087	15	1		63	144	25	1400	3	1	
19	886	20	1103	16			64	169	25	1397	3		
20	+ 867	19	+1118	15			65	—194	—24	+1394	— 3		
21	847	—20	1133	+13	1		66	218	25	1391	4	1	
22	826	21	1147	14			67	243	25	1387	5		
23	806	20	1161	14			68	268	24	1382	5		
24	785	21	1175	14	1		69	292	26	1377	5	—1	
25	764	21	1188	13			70	317	24	1372	6		
26	743	22	1201	13			71	341	24	1367	6		
27	721	22	1214	13	1		72	365	24	1361	6	0	
28	700	21	1226	13			73	389	24	1354	7		
29	678	22	1238	13			74	413	24	1347	7		
30	+ 656	22	+1249	11	1		75	—437	—24	+1340	— 7	0	
31	634	—22	1260	+11			76	461	24	1333	7		
32	611	23	1271	11			77	485	24	1325	8		
33	588	23	1281	10	1		78	508	23	1316	9	0	
34	565	23	1291	10			79	531	23	1307	9		
35	542	23	1301	10			80	555	24	1298	9		
36	519	23	1310	0	1		81	578	23	1288	10	0	
37	496	23	1319	9			82	600	22	1278	10		
38	472	24	1327	8			83	623	23	1268	10		
39	448	24	1335	8	1		84	645	22	1257	11	0	
40	+ 425	25	+1343	8			85	—669	—22	+1245	12		
41	401	—24	1350	+ 7			86	690	22	1233	—12		
42	377	24	1356	6	1		87	712	22	1221	12	0	
43	353	24	1363	7			88	733	21	1209	13		
44	329	26	1369	6			89	755	22	1197	12		
45	+ 304	—24	+1374	+ 5	—1		90	—776	—21	+1184	—13	0	

TABLE IV. — *Continued.*

PERTURBATIONS OF THE CO-ORDINATES IN UNITS OF THE SIXTH DECIMAL.
ARGUMENT V.

Arg.	ξ	Diff.	η'	Diff.	ζ	Diff.	Arg.	ξ	Diff.	η'	Diff.	ζ	Diff.
90	−776	−21	+1184	−14	0		135	−1399	−6	+297	−24	+1	
91	797	20	1170	14			136	1404	6	273	24		
92	817	21	1156	14			137	1409	4	249	24		
93	838	20	1142	14	0		138	1413	4	225	21	1	
94	858	20	1123	15			139	1417	8	201	23		
95	879	19	1113	16			140	1420	3	176	24		
96	897	20	1097	15	0		141	1423	3	152	26	1	
97	917	19	1082	16			142	1426	2	127	24		
98	936	19	1066	16			143	1428	1	103	25		
99	955	18	1050	17	0		144	1429	1	78	24	1	
100	−973	−18	+1033	−17			145	−1430	−1	+54	−25		
101	991	18	1016	17			146	1431	0	29	24		
102	1009	18	999	17	0		147	1431	0	+5	25	1	
103	1027	17	982	18			148	1431	+1	−20	21		
104	1044	17	964	18			149	1430	1	44	25		
105	1061	17	946	18	0		150	1429	1	69	24	1	
106	1078	16	928	19			151	1428	2	93	25		
107	1094	16	909	19			152	1426	2	118	24		
108	1110	16	890	19	0		153	1424	3	142	25	1	
109	1126	15	871	20			154	1421	8	167	24		
110	−1141	−13	+851	−19			155	−1418	+4	−191	−23		
111	1156	14	832	20	+1		156	1414	4	215	25	1	
112	1170	15	812	21			157	1410	5	240	24		
113	1185	14	791	20			158	1405	6	264	24		
114	1199	13	771	21	1		159	1400	5	288	24	1	
115	1212	13	750	21			160	1395	6	312	24		
116	1225	13	729	21			161	1389	6	336	24		
117	1238	12	708	21	1		162	1383	7	360	23	1	
118	1250	12	687	22			163	1376	7	383	24		
119	1262	12	665	21			164	1369	7	407	23		
120	−1274	−11	+644	−22	1		165	−1362	+8	−430	−23	1	
121	1285	11	622	23			166	1354	8	453	24		
122	1296	10	599	22			167	1346	9	477	23		
123	1306	10	577	22	1		168	1337	9	500	22	2	
124	1316	10	555	23			169	1328	10	522	23		
125	1326	9	532	23			170	1318	10	545	23		
126	1335	9	509	23	1		171	1308	10	568	22	2	
127	1344	8	486	23			172	1298	11	590	22		
128	1352	8	463	23			173	1287	11	612	22		
129	1360	8	440	24	1		174	1276	11	634	22	2	
130	−1368	−7	+416	−23			175	−1265	+12	−656	−21		
131	1375	7	393	24			176	1253	12	677	23		
132	1382	6	369	24	1		177	1241	13	699	21	2	
133	1388	6	345	24			178	1228	13	720	21		
134	1394	−5	321	24			179	1215	12	741	21		
135	−1399		+297	−24	+1		180	−1202		−762	−21	+2	

TABLE IV. — *Continued.*

PERTURBATIONS OF THE CO-ORDINATES IN UNITS OF THE SIXTH DECIMAL.
ARGUMENT V.

Arg	ξ'	Diff.	η'	Diff.	ζ'	Diff.	Arg	ξ'	Diff.	η'	Diff.	ζ'	Diff.
°							°						
180	−1292	+14	−763	−20	+2		225	−301	+24	−1372	−5	+1	
181	1188	14	782	20			226	277	24	1377		−5	
182	1174	11	802	20			227	252	25	1382	5		
183	1159	15	822	20	2		228	228	24	1386	4	1	
184	1144	15	842	20			229	203	25	1389	3		
185	1129	15	862	20			230	178	25	1392	3		
186	1114	15	881	19	2		231	154	24	1395	3	1	
187	1098	16	900	19			232	129	25	1398	3		
188	1082	16	918	18			233	104	25	1400	2		
189	1065	17	937	19	2		234	79	25	1402	2	1	
		17		19					25		1		
190	−1048	+17	−955	−18			235	−54	+25	−1403	0		
191	1031	17	973	17			236	29	25	1403	0		
192	1014	17	990	17	2		237	−4	25	1404	−1	1	
193	996	18	1007	17			238	+21	25	1404	0		
194	978	18	1024	17			239	46	25	1403	+1		
195	959	19	1041	17	2		240	70	24	1402	1	1	
196	941	16	1057	16			241	95	25	1401	1		
197	922	19	1073	16			242	120	25	1399	2		
198	903	19	1089	16	1		243	145	25	1396	3	1	
199	883	20	1104	15			244	170	25	1394	2		
		20		15					24		3		
200	−863	+20	−1119	−15			245	+194	+25	−1391	3		
201	843	20	1134	−13	1		246	219	25	1387	+4	1	
202	823	20	1148	14			247	244	25	1383	4		
203	803	20	1162	14			248	268	24	1379	4		
204	782	21	1175	13	1		249	292	24	1374	5	1	
205	761	21	1188	13			250	317	25	1369	5		
206	740	21	1201	13			251	341	24	1363	6		
207	718	22	1214	13	1		252	365	24	1357	6	+1	
208	696	22	1226	12			253	380	24	1351	6		
209	674	22	1238	12			254	413	24	1344	7		
		22		11					24		6		
210	−652	+22	−1249	−11	1		255	+437	+24	−1336	6	0	
211	630	22	1260	11			256	461	24	1329	+7		
212	608	23	1271	11			257	484	23	1321	8		
213	585	23	1281	10	1		258	508	24	1312	9	0	
214	562	23	1291	10			259	531	23	1303	9		
215	539	23	1300	9			260	554	23	1294	9		
216	516	23	1309	9	1		261	577	23	1284	10	0	
217	492	24	1318	0			262	599	23	1274	10		
218	469	23	1326	8			263	622	23	1264	10		
219	445	24	1334	8	1		264	644	22	1253	11	0	
		23		7					22		11		
220	−422	+24	−1341				265	+666	+22	−1242	11		
221	398	24	1348	−7			266	688	22	1230	+12		
222	374	24	1355	7	1		267	710	22	1218	12	0	
223	359	24	1361	6			268	731	21	1206	12		
224	325	25	1367	6			269	753	22	1193	13		
225	−301	+24	−1372	−5	+1		270	+774	+21	−1180	+13	0	

TABLE IV.— *Continued.*
PERTURBATIONS OF THE CO-ORDINATES IN UNITS OF THE SIXTH DECIMAL.
ARGUMENT V.

Arg.	ξ'	Diff.	η'	Diff.	ζ	Diff.	Arg.	ξ'	Diff.	η'	Diff.	ζ	Diff.
° 270	+774		-1180		0		° 315	+1397		-299		-1	
271	795	+21	1167	+13			316	1402	+5	275	+24		
272	815	20	1153	14			317	1406	6	251	24		
273	835	20	1139	14	0		318	1411	5	227	24	1	
274	855	20	1125	14			319	1415	4	203	24		
275	875	20	1110	15			320	1418	3	179	24		
276	895	20	1095	15	0		321	1421	3	154	25	1	
277	914	19	1079	16			322	1423	2	130	24		
278	933	19	1063	16			323	1425	2	106	24		
279	952	19	1047	16	0		324	1427	2	81	25	1	
		18		16					1		24		
280	+970		-1031				325	+1428		-57			
281	988	+18	1014	+17			326	1429	+1	32	+25		
282	1006	18	997	17	0		327	1430	+1	-8	24	1	
283	1024	18	980	17			328	1430	0	+17	25		
284	1041	17	962	18			329	1429	-1	41	24		
285	1058	17	944	18	0		330	1428	1	66	25	1	
286	1075	17	926	18			331	1427	1	90	24		
287	1091	16	907	19			332	1425	2	114	24		
288	1107	16	889	18	-1		333	1423	2	139	25	1	
289	1122	15	870	19			334	1420	3	163	24		
		16		20					3		25		
290	+1138		-850				335	+1417		+188			
291	1153	+15	831	+19	1		336	1413	-4	212	+24	1	
292	1167	14	811	20			337	1409	4	236	24		
293	1181	14	791	20			338	1405	4	260	24		
294	1195	14	770	21	1		339	1400	5	284	24	1	
295	1209	14	750	20			340	1395	5	308	24		
296	1222	13	729	21			341	1389	6	332	24		
297	1234	12	708	21	1		342	1383	6	356	24	1	
298	1247	13	687	21			343	1377	6	379	23		
299	1259	12	665	22			344	1370	7	403	24		
		11		21					8		23		
300	+1270		-644		1		345	+1362		+426		1	
301	1282	+12	622	+22			346	1354	-8	450	+24		
302	1293	11	600	22			347	1346	8	473	23		
303	1303	10	578	22	1		348	1338	8	496	23	2	
304	1313	10	555	23			349	1329	9	519	23		
305	1323	10	533	22			350	1319	10	541	22		
306	1332	9	510	23	1		351	1309	10	564	23	2	
307	1341	9	487	23			352	1299	10	586	22		
308	1349	8	464	23			353	1289	10	609	23		
309	1357	8	441	23	1		354	1278	11	631	22	2	
		8		23					12		21		
310	+1365		-418				355	+1266		+652			
311	1372	+7	394	+24			356	1254	-12	674	+22		
312	1379	7	371	23	1		357	1242	12	695	21	2	
313	1385	6	347	24			358	1230	12	717	22		
314	1391	6	323	24			359	1217	13	738	21		
315	+1397	+6	-299	24	-1		360	+1204	-13	+758	+20	-2	

50

TABLE IV.— *Continued.*

PERTURBATIONS OF THE CO-ORDINATES IN UNITS OF THE SIXTH DECIMAL.
ARGUMENT VI.

Arg.	ξ'	Diff.	η'	Diff.	ζ'	Diff.	Arg.	ξ'	Diff.	η'	Diff.	ζ'	Diff.
0	+1041		-143		-505		45	+1010		+ 856		+ 14	
		+ 6		+23		+ 9			- 8		+18		+12
1	1047		120		496		46	1002		874		26	
		6		23		10			8		19		13
2	1053		97		486		47	993		893		39	
		6		23		0			9		18		12
3	1059		74		477		48	984		911		51	
		6		23		10			9		18		13
4	1065		51		467		49	975		929		64	
		5		24		10			9		18		12
5	1070		27		457		50	966		947		76	
		5		23		10			9		17		13
6	1075		- 4		447		51	956		964		89	
		4		23		10			10		17		13
7	1079		+ 10		437		52	946		981		101	
		4		24		11			10		17		13
8	1083		43		426		53	936		998		114	
		4		23		10			11		17		13
9	1087		66		416		54	925		1015		126	
		4		24		11			11		16		12
10	+1091		+ 90		-405		55	+ 914		+1031		+138	
		+ 3		+23		+10			-11		+16		+12
11	1094		113		395		56	903		1047		150	
		3		23		11			11		16		13
12	1097		136		384		57	892		1063		163	
		3		24		11			11		16		13
13	1100		160		373		58	880		1078		175	
		2		23		11			12		15		12
14	1102		183		362		59	868		1093		187	
		2		23		11			12		14		12
15	1104		206		351		60	856		1107		199	
		2		24		11			12		15		12
16	1106		230		340		61	843		1122		211	
		2		23		11			13		15		12
17	1107		253		328		62	830		1136		223	
		1		23		12			13		14		12
18	1108		276		317		63	817		1149		235	
		1		23		11			13		13		12
19	1109		299		306		64	804		1162		247	
		+ 1		23		12			13		13		12
20	+1109		+322		-294		65	+ 791		+1175		+258	
		0		+23		+12			-14		+13		+12
21	1109		345		282		66	777		1188		270	
		0		23		12			14		13		12
22	1109		368		270		67	763		1200		281	
		- 1		23		11			15		12		11
23	1108		391		259		68	748		1212		293	
		1		23		12			14		11		11
24	1107		414		247		69	734		1223		304	
		1		22		12			15		11		11
25	1106		436		235		70	719		1234		315	
		1		23		12			15		11		12
26	1104		459		223		71	704		1245		327	
		2		22		12			16		10		11
27	1102		481		211		72	688		1255		338	
		2		22		13			15		10		11
28	1100		503		198		73	673		1265		349	
		3		22		12			16		9		10
29	1097		525		186		74	657		1274		359	
		3		22		12			16		9		11
30	+1094		+547		-174		75	+ 641		+1283		+370	
		- 3		+22		+12			-16		+ 9		+11
31	1091		569		162		76	625		1292		381	
		4		23		13			16		8		10
32	1087		591		149		77	609		1300		391	
		4		21		12			17		8		11
33	1083		612		137		78	592		1308		402	
		4		22		12			17		7		10
34	1079		634		125		79	575		1315		412	
		5		21		13			17		7		10
35	1074		655		112		80	558		1322		422	
		5		21		12			17		6		10
36	1069		676		100		81	541		1328		432	
		5		21		13			17		6		10
37	1064		697		87		82	524		1334		442	
		6		20		13			17		6		10
38	1058		717		74		83	507		1340		452	
		6		21		12			18		5		0
39	1052		738		62		84	489		1345		461	
		6		20		13			18		5		10
40	+1046		+758		- 49		85	+ 471		+1350		+471	
		- 7		+20		+12			-18		+ 5		+ 9
41	1039		778		37		86	453		1355		480	
		7		20		13			18		4		9
42	1032		798		24		87	435		1359		489	
		7		19		13			18		3		9
43	1025		817		- 12		88	417		1362		498	
		7		20		13			18		3		9
44	1018		837		+ 1		89	399		1365		507	
		- 8		+19		+13			-19		+ 3		+ 9
45	+1010		+856		+ 14		90	+ 380		+1369		+516	

TABLE ·IV.— *Continued.*

PERTURBATIONS OF THE CO-ORDINATES IN UNITS THE SIXTH DECIMAL.

ARGUMENT VI.

Arg.	ξ'	Diff.	η'	Diff.	ζ'	Diff.	Arg.	ξ'	Diff.	η'	Diff.	ζ'	Diff.
90	+380	-19	+1368	+2	+516	+9	135	-492	-19	+1042	-17	+720	-1
91	361	18	1370	2	525	8	136	510	18	1025	16	719	0
92	343	19	1372	2	533	8	137	528	18	1009	16	719	0
93	324	19	1373	1	541	8	138	546	18	992	17	718	1
94	305	19	1374	+1	549	8	139	563	17	975	17	718	0
95	286	19	1374	0	557	8	140	580	17	958	17	717	1
96	266	20	1374	0	565	8	141	597	17	940	18	716	1
97	247	19	1374	0	573	8	142	614	17	922	18	714	2
98	228	19	1373	-1	580	7	143	631	17	904	18	713	1
99	208	20	1371	2	587	7	144	648	17	885	19	711	2
		19		2		7			16		19		2
100	+189	-20	+1369	-2	+594	+7	145	-664	-18	+866	-19	+709	-3
101	169	19	1367	2	601	7	146	680	16	847	19	706	2
102	150	20	1365	2	608	7	147	696	15	828	20	704	3
103	130	20	1362	3	615	7	148	711	16	808	20	701	3
104	110	20	1358	4	621	6	149	727	15	788	20	698	3
105	90	20	1354	4	627	6	150	742	15	768	20	695	3
106	70	20	1350	4	633	6	151	757	15	748	20	692	3
107	50	20	1345	5	639	6	152	772	14	727	21	688	4
108	31	19	1339	6	644	5	153	786	14	706	21	684	4
109	+11	20	1333	6	650	6	154	800	14	685	21	680	4
		20		6		5			14		21		4
110	-9	-20	+1327	-6	+655	+5	155	-814	-14	+664	-21	+676	-4
111	29	20	1321	7	660	5	156	828	13	643	22	672	5
112	49	20	1314	8	665	5	157	841	14	621	22	667	4
113	69	20	1306	8	670	5	158	855	13	599	22	663	5
114	89	20	1298	8	674	4	159	868	12	577	22	658	5
115	109	20	1290	9	678	4	160	880	12	555	22	653	6
116	129	20	1281	9	682	4	161	892	12	533	22	647	5
117	149	19	1272	9	686	4	162	904	12	511	22	642	6
118	168	20	1263	10	690	3	163	916	12	488	23	636	6
119	188	20	1253	11	693	4	164	928	11	466	23	630	6
		20		11		4			11		23		6
120	-208	-19	+1242	-10	+697	+3	165	-939	-11	+443	-23	+624	-7
121	227	20	1232	11	700	2	166	950	10	420	23	617	6
122	247	20	1221	12	702	3	167	960	11	397	23	611	7
123	267	19	1209	12	705	2	168	971	10	374	24	604	7
124	286	19	1197	12	707	3	169	981	9	350	23	597	7
125	305	20	1185	13	710	2	170	990	10	327	23	590	7
126	325	19	1172	13	712	1	171	1000	9	304	24	583	7
127	344	19	1159	13	713	2	172	1009	9	280	23	576	8
128	363	18	1146	14	715	1	173	1018	8	257	24	568	8
129	381	19	1132	14	716	1	174	1026	8	233	23	560	8
		19		14		1			8		23		8
130	-400	-19	+1118	-15	+717	+1	175	-1034	-8	+210	-24	+552	-8
131	419	18	1103	15	718	1	176	1042	7	186	24	544	8
132	437	19	1088	15	719	0	177	1049	7	162	24	536	8
133	456	18	1073	15	719	+1	178	1056	7	138	23	528	9
134	474	18	1058	16	720	0	179	1063	6	115	24	519	9
135	-492		+1042		+720		180	-1069		+91		+510	

TABLE IV. — *Continued.*

PERTURBATIONS OF THE CO-ORDINATES IN UNITS OF THE SIXTH DECIMAL.
ARGUMENT VI.

Arg.	ξ'	Diff.	η'	Diff.	ζ'	Diff.	Arg.	ξ'	Diff.	η'	Diff.	ζ'	Diff.
180	-1069	-6	+91	-24	+510	-9	225	-1000	+9	-876	-17	-2	-13
181	1075	6	67	24	501	9	226	991	10	893	17	15	13
182	1081	5	43	23	492	9	227	981	10	910	16	28	13
183	1086	5	+20	24	483	10	228	971	10	926	16	40	12
184	1091	6	-4	24	473	9	229	961	10	942	16	53	13
185	1096	4	28	24	464	10	230	951	10	958	16	66	13
186	1100	4	52	23	454	10	231	941	11	974	15	78	12
187	1104	4	75	24	444	10	232	930	12	989	15	91	13
188	1108	3	99	28	434	10	233	918	11	1004	15	104	13
189	1111	3	122	24	424	10	234	907	12	1018	14	117	13
190	-1114	-3	-146	-23	+414	-10	235	-895	+12	-1033	-14	-129	-13
191	1117	2	169	24	404	11	236	883	12	1047	13	142	12
192	1119	2	193	23	393	11	237	871	12	1060	14	154	12
193	1121	1	216	23	383	10	238	859	13	1074	14	167	13
194	1122	1	239	23	372	11	239	846	13	1087	13	179	12
195	1123	1	262	23	361	11	240	833	13	1099	12	192	13
196	1124	-1	285	23	350	11	241	820	13	1111	12	204	12
197	1125	0	308	23	339	11	242	807	13	1123	12	216	12
198	1125	0	331	23	328	11	243	793	14	1135	12	228	12
199	1125	+1	353	22	317	11	244	779	14	1146	11	241	13
200	-1124	+1	-376	-23	+305	-12	245	-765	+14	-1157	-11	-253	-12
201	1123	1	398	22	294	11	246	750	15	1168	11	265	12
202	1122	2	420	22	282	12	247	736	14	1178	10	277	12
203	1120	2	442	22	271	11	248	721	15	1188	10	288	12
204	1118	2	464	22	259	12	249	706	15	1198	10	300	12
205	1116	2	486	22	247	12	250	691	15	1207	9	312	12
206	1113	3	507	21	235	12	251	676	15	1216	9	324	11
207	1110	3	529	22	223	12	252	660	16	1225	9	335	11
208	1107	3	550	21	211	12	253	644	16	1233	8	346	11
209	1103	4	571	21	199	12	254	628	16	1241	8	358	12
210	-1099	+4	-592	-20	+187	-13	255	-612	+16	-1248	-7	-369	-11
211	1095	5	612	21	174	12	256	596	17	1255	7	380	11
212	1090	6	633	21	162	12	257	579	16	1262	7	391	11
213	1085	6	653	20	150	12	258	563	17	1268	6	402	11
214	1080	6	673	20	137	13	259	546	17	1274	6	412	10
215	1074	6	692	19	125	12	260	529	17	1280	6	423	11
216	1068	6	712	20	112	13	261	512	17	1285	5	433	10
217	1062	7	731	19	100	13	262	495	17	1290	5	444	11
218	1055	7	750	19	87	13	263	477	18	1294	4	454	10
219	1048	7	760	19	74	13	264	460	17	1298	4	464	10
220	-1041	+8	-787	-19	+62	-13	265	-442	+18	-1302	-4	-474	-10
221	1033	8	806	18	49	13	266	424	18	1306	3	484	10
222	1025	8	824	18	36	12	267	406	18	1309	2	493	10
223	1017	8	842	17	24	12	268	388	18	1311	2	503	9
224	1009	+9	859	-17	+11	-13	269	370	18	1313	-2	512	-9
225	-1000		-876		-2		270	-352	+18	-1315		-521	

TABLE IV.— Continued.

PERTURBATIONS OF THE CO-ORDINATES IN UNITS OF THE SIXTH DECIMAL.

ARGUMENT VI.

Arg.	ξ'	Diff.	η'	Diff.	ζ'	Diff.	Arg.	ξ'	Diff.	η'	Diff.	ζ'	Diff.
270	-352	+18	-1315	-2	-521	-0	315	+482	+17	-1021	+4	-731	+0
271	334	19	1317		530		316	499	17	1007	4	731	1
272	315	18	1318	1	539	0	317	516	17	992	5	730	0
273	297	10	1319	-1	548	0	318	533	17	977	5	730	0
274	278	10	1319	0	556	8	319	549	16	962	5	729	1
275	260	18	1319	0	564	8	320	566	17	946	6	727	2
276	241	19	1319	0	572	8	321	582	16	930	6	726	1
277	222	10	1318	+1	580	8	322	598	16	914	6	724	2
278	204	18	1317	1	588	8	323	614	18	808	6	722	2
279	185	19	1315	2	596	8	324	629	16	881	7	720	2
		19		2		7			16		7		2
280	-166	+19	-1313	+2	-603	-8	325	+645	+15	-864	+7	-718	+3
281	147	19	1311	2	611	7	326	660	15	847	7	715	3
282	128	19	1308	3	618	6	327	675	15	830	7	712	3
283	109	19	1305	3	624	6	328	690	15	812	8	709	3
284	90	19	1302	3	631	7	329	705	15	794	8	706	3
285	71	10	1298	4	637	8	330	719	14	776	8	703	3
286	52	19	1294	4	644	7	331	734	15	758	8	699	4
287	33	19	1290	4	650	6	332	748	14	739	9	695	4
288	-14	19	1285	5	655	5	333	762	14	720	9	691	4
289	+5	19	1280	5	661	6	334	775	13	701	9	686	4
		19		6		6			14		9		4
290	+24	+19	-1274	+6	-667	-5	335	+789	+13	-682	+9	-682	+5
291	43	19	1268	6	672	5	336	802	13	662	10	677	5
292	62	19	1262	6	677	5	337	815	13	643	9	672	5
293	81	19	1255	7	682	5	338	828	13	623	10	667	5
294	100	19	1248	7	686	4	339	840	12	603	10	662	5
295	119	19	1241	7	691	5	340	852	12	582	11	656	6
296	138	19	1233	8	695	4	341	864	12	562	10	650	6
297	157	19	1225	8	699	4	342	876	12	541	11	644	6
298	176	19	1216	9	702	3	343	888	12	520	11	638	6
299	195	19	1207	9	706	4	344	899	11	499	11	632	6
		18		9		3			11		11		7
300	+213	+19	-1198	+9	-709	-3	345	+910	+10	-478	-12	-625	+7
301	232	18	1189	10	712	3	346	920	11	456	11	618	7
302	250	19	1179	10	715	3	347	931	11	435	11	611	7
303	269	19	1169	10	718	3	348	941	10	413	12	604	7
304	287	13	1158	11	720	2	349	951	10	391	12	597	7
305	305	18	1147	11	722	2	350	961	10	369	12	589	8
306	324	19	1136	11	724	2	351	970	9	347	12	582	7
307	342	13	1125	11	726	2	352	979	9	325	12	574	8
308	360	18	1113	12	727	1	353	988	0	303	12	566	8
309	378	18	1101	12	729	2	354	996	8	280	13	558	8
		17		13		1			8		13		9
310	+395	+18	-1088	+13	-730		355	+1004	+8	-257	+12	-549	+8
311	413	18	1075	13	730	0	356	1012	8	235	13	541	8
312	431	16	1062	13	731	-1	357	1020	8	212	13	532	9
313	448	17	1049	13	731	0	358	1027	7	189	13	523	0
314	465	17	1035	14	731	0	359	1034	7	166	13	514	9
315	+482	+17	-1021	+14	-731	-0	360	+1041	+7	-143	+13	-505	+9

54

TABLE IV. — *Continued.*
PERTURBATIONS OF THE CO-ORDINATES IN UNITS OF THE SIXTH DECIMAL.
ARGUMENT VII.

Arg.	ξ'	Diff.	η'	Diff.	ζ'	Diff.	Arg.	ξ'	Diff.	η'	Diff.	ζ'	Diff.
0	− 300	− 26	+ 18	0	+80	−3	180	+939	− 54	+387	+104	−80	+3
5	326	31	18	− 7	77	3	185	885	67	491	96	77	3
10	357	33	+ 11	15	74	4	190	818	79	587	85	74	4
15	390	34	− 4	25	70	5	195	739	88	672	75	70	5
20	424	33	29	34	65	5	200	651	97	747	75	65	5
25	457	30	63	43	60	5	205	554	102	809	62	60	5
30	487	24	106	51	55	5	210	452	107	857	48	55	6
35	511	17	157	60	49	6	215	345	109	892	35	49	8
40	528	− 9	217	66	43	6	220	236	109	912	20	43	8
45	537	+ 2	283	71	36	7	225	127	107	917	+ 5	36	7
50	− 535	+ 13	−354	− 71	+29	7	230	+ 20	−102	+908	− 23	−29	7
55	522	26	428	73	22	−7	235	− 82	96	885	36	22	+7
60	496	37	503	75	15	7	240	178	88	849	36	15	7
65	459	50	577	74	+ 7	8	245	266	88	802	47	− 7	8
70	409	62	647	70	0	7	250	345	79	744	58	0	7
75	347	73	712	65	− 7	7	255	412	67	679	65	+ 7	7
80	274	83	770	58	15	8	260	467	55	607	72	15	8
85	191	92	819	49	22	7	265	510	43	531	76	22	7
90	99	98	858	39	29	7	270	540	30	453	76	29	7
95	− 1	103	884	26	36	7	275	558	16	375	76	36	7
100	+ 102	+103	−897	− 13	−43	7	280	−563	− 5	+300	75	+43	7
105	208	107	896	+ 1	49	−6	285	558	+ 5	229	− 71	49	+6
110	315	106	881	15	55	6	290	542	16	163	66	55	6
115	421	103	852	29	60	5	295	519	22	106	57	60	5
120	524	97	809	43	65	5	300	489	30	57	49	65	5
125	621	90	752	57	70	5	305	455	34	+ 17	40	70	5
130	711	81	682	70	74	4	310	419	36	− 13	30	74	4
135	792	71	601	81	77	3	315	383	36	34	21	77	3
140	863	59	509	92	80	3	320	349	34	45	11	80	3
145	922	46	408	101	82	2	325	318	31	49	− 4	82	2
150	+ 968	+ 32	−301	107	−84	2	330	−293	25	− 46	+ 3	+84	2
155	1000	17	188	+113	85	−1	335	275	+ 16	37	+ 9	85	+1
160	1017	+ 3	− 72	116	85	0	340	264	11	25	14	85	0
165	1020	− 13	+ 46	116	65	0	345	261	+ 3	− 12	13	85	0
170	1007	27	163	117	64	+1	350	266	− 5	+ 1	13	84	−1
175	980	− 41	277	114	82	2	355	279	13	12	11	82	2
180	+ 939		+387	110	−80	+2	360	−300	− 21	+ 18	+ 6	+80	−2

TABLE IV. — *Continued.*

PERTURBATIONS OF THE CO-ORDINATES IN UNITS OF THE SIXTH DECIMAL.
ARGUMENT VIII.

Arg.	ζ'	Diff.	η'	Diff.	ζ'	Diff.	Arg.	ζ'	Diff.	η'	Diff.	ζ'	Diff.
°							°						
0	+ 107	+ 7	− 13	+ 3	−61		180	-340	+25	+174	+35	+66	
5	114		10		50	+2	185	315		209		63	− 3
10	123	9	10	0	57	2	190	287	28	240	31	60	3
15	134	11	13	− 3	54	3	195	255	32	268	26	57	3
20	145	11	20	7	51	3	200	220	35	292	21	53	4
25	157	12	30	10	48	3	205	183	37	311	19	49	4
30	168	11	44	14	44	4	210	145	38	326	15	44	5
35	177	9	63	15	40	4	215	105	40	335	9	39	5
40	184	7	84	21	36	4	220	66	39	340	+ 5	34	5
45	187	+ 3	109	25	32	4	225	− 27	39	340	0	28	6
		0		27		5			38		− 4		5
50	+ 187	− 4	−136	− 29	−27	+5	230	+ 11	+37	+336	− 8	+23	−6
55	193	0	165	30	22	5	235	48		328		17	6
60	174	0	195	30	16	6	240	82	34	315	13	11	6
65	160	11	224	29	11	5	245	113	31	298	17	+ 5	6
70	141	18	253	29	− 5	6	250	141	29	278	20	− 1	6
75	117	24	270	26	+ 1	6	255	165	24	255	23	7	6
80	89	29	302	28	7	6	260	185	20	230	25	13	6
85	55	33	321	19	13	6	265	201	16	202	28	18	5
90	+ 19	36	335	14	18	5	270	213	12	174	28	23	5
95	− 20	39	344	9	24	6	275	220	7	145	29	28	5
		40		− 8		6			+ 4		29		5
100	− 60	−42	−347	+ 3	+30	+5	280	+224	− 1	+116	−27	−33	−5
105	102	42	344	3	35	5	285	223		89		38	4
110	144	41	335	9	40	5	290	219	4	63	26	42	4
115	185	39	320	15	45	5	295	211	8	39	24	46	4
120	224	36	299	21	50	5	300	201	10	+ 18	21	50	4
125	260	33	272	27	54	.4	305	189	12	0	18	53	3
130	293	29	241	31	58	4	310	175	14	− 15	15	55	2
135	322	24	206	35	61	3	315	162	13	26	11	58	3
140	346	19	167	39	64	3	320	148	14	33	7	60	2
145	365	14	125	42	66	2	325	135	13	37	4	61	1
		11		43		2			12		− 1		1
150	− 379	− 7	− 82	+ 43	+68	+1	330	+123	− 9	− 38	+ 1	−62	−1
155	386	− 2	− 37	45	69	0	335	114		37		63	1
160	398	+ 4	+ 8	44	69	0	340	107	7	33	4	63	0
165	384	10	52	42	69	0	345	102	6	28	5	63	0
170	374	15	94	41	69	0	350	101	− 1	22	6	63	0
175	359	+19	135	+ 39	68	−1	355	103	+ 2	17	5	62	+1
180	− 340		+174		+66	−2	360	+107	+ 4	− 13	+ 4	−61	+1

TABLE IV. — *Continued.*

PERTURBATIONS OF THE CO-ORDINATES IN UNITS OF THE SIXTH DECIMAL.

ARGUMENT IX.

Arg.	ξ'	Diff.	η'	Diff.	ζ'	Diff.	Arg.	ξ'	Diff.	η'	Diff.	ζ'	Diff.
0	+183	+1	-22	+27	+7	+2	180	-217	+1	-22	-7	+113	0
5	184		+5	26	9	1	185	216		29	7	113	0
10	181	-3	31	26	10	2	190	215	1	36	7	112	-1
15	174	7	57	26	12	8	195	213	2	44	8	112	0
20	164	10	81	24	15	8	200	211	2	51	7	111	1
25	150	14	104	23	19	4	205	209	2	58	7	110	1
30	134	16	124	20	24	5	210	207	2	66	8	108	2
35	116	18	142	13	29	5	215	204	3	74	8	107	1
40	95	21	157	13	35	6	220	200	4	82	8	106	1
45	73	22	169	13	41	6	225	196	4	90	8	104	2
50	+50	23	+178	9	+47	6	230	-192	4	-99	-9	+102	2
55	26	-24	184	+6	53	+8	235	186	+6	108	9	100	-2
60	+2	24	188	+4	59	6	240	180	6	117	9	98	2
65	-21	23	188	0	64	5	245	173	7	126	9	96	2
70	44	23	186	-2	70	6	250	164	9	135	9	93	3
75	65	21	182	4	75	5	255	155	9	145	10	90	3
80	85	20	176	6	80	5	260	144	11	154	9	87	3
85	104	19	168	8	85	5	265	132	12	163	9	84	3
90	121	17	159	9	89	4	270	119	13	172	8	80	4
95	137	16	149	10	92	3	275	104	15	180	8	76	4
100	-151	14	+138	11	+96	4	280	-88	16	-187	7	+71	5
105	163	-12	126	-12	99	+3	285	71	+17	193	-6	67	-4
110	174	11	114	13	101	2	290	53	18	198	5	62	5
115	183	9	102	14	104	3	295	33	20	201	3	57	5
120	191	8	90	12	106	2	300	-13	20	202	-1	51	6
125	198	7	78	12	107	1	305	+8	21	201	+1	46	5
130	203	5	67	11	109	2	310	30	22	198	3	40	6
135	208	5	56	11	110	1	315	52	22	192	6	34	6
140	211	8	46	10	111	1	320	73	21	183	9	29	5
145	214	3	36	10	112	1	325	94	21	171	12	24	5
150	-216	2	+26	10	+113	1	330	+113	19	-156	15	+20	4
155	217	-1	17	-9	113	0	335	131	+18	139	+17	16	-4
160	218	-1	+8	9	114	+1	340	147	16	119	20	12	4
165	218	0	0	8	114	0	345	161	14	97	22	10	2
170	218	0	-7	7	114	0	350	172	11	73	24	8	2
175	218	0	15	8	114	0	355	179	7	48	25	7	-1
180	-217	+1	-22	-7	+113	-1	360	+183	+4	-22	+26	+7	0

TABLE IV. — *Continued.*

PERTURBATIONS OF THE CO-ORDINATES IN UNITS OF THE SIXTH DECIMAL.

ARGUMENT X.

Arg.	ξ'	Diff.	η'	Diff.	ζ'	Diff.	Arg.	ξ'	Diff.	η'	Diff.	ζ'	Diff.
0	-139	+3	-38	-10	+8		180	+178	-7	+62	+16	-8	
5	136	+3	48	-11		-1	185	171	-9	78	+16		+1
10	133	+4	59	-10	7		190	162	-11	94	+14	7	
15	129	+5	69	-11		-1	195	151	-12	108	+13		+1
20	124	+5	80	-10	6		200	139	-14	121	+12	6	
25	119	+6	90	-10		-1	205	125	-14	133	+11		+1
30	113	+7	100	-10	5		210	111	-16	144	+8	5	
35	106	+8	110	-9		-1	215	95	-16	152	+7		+1
40	98	+9	119	-9	4		220	79	-16	159	+6	4	
45	89	+10	128	-9		-1	225	63	-16	165	+4		+1
50	-79	+11	-137	-7	+3		230	+47	-17	+169	+2	-3	
55	68	+11	144	-7		-2	235	30	-16	171	0		+2
60	57	+13	151	-6	+1		240	+14	-16	171	-1	-1	
65	44	+14	157	-5		-1	245	-2	-15	170	-2		+1
70	30	+14	162	-4	0		250	17	-15	168	-4	0	
75	16	+15	166	-3		-2	255	32	-14	164	-5		+2
80	-1	+16	169	-1	-2		260	46	-13	159	-6	+2	
85	+15	+16	170	+1		-1	265	59	-12	153	-7		+1
90	31	+16	169	+2	3		270	71	-11	146	-8	3	
95	47	+16	167	+3		-2	275	82	-10	138	-9		+2
100	+63	+16	-164	+5	-5		280	-92	-9	+129	-9	+5	
105	79	+16	159	+7		-1	285	101	-8	120	-10		+1
110	95	+15	152	+9	6		290	109	-7	110	-10	6	
115	110	+14	143	+10		-1	295	116	-6	100	-10		+1
120	124	+14	133	+11	7		300	122	-5	90	-11	7	
125	138	+12	122	+13		-1	305	127	-4	79	-10		+1
130	150	+11	109	+14	8		310	131	-4	69	-11	8	
135	161	+9	95	+16		0	315	135	-3	58	-11		0
140	170	+8	79	+16	8		320	138	-2	47	-11	8	
145	178	+6	63	+17		0	325	140	-1	36	-10		0
150	+184	+4	-46	+18	-8		330	-141	-1	+26	-11	+8	
155	188	+2	28	+18		-1	335	142	0	15	-11		+1
160	190	0	-10	+18	9		340	142	0	+4	-10	9	
165	190	-2	+8	+18	+1		345	142	+1	-6	-11		-1
170	188	-4	26	+18	8		350	141	+1	17	-10	8	
175	184	-6	44	+18		0	355	140	+2	27	-11		0
180	+178		+62		-8		360	-138		-38		+8	

TABLE IV. — *Continued.*

PERTURBATIONS OF THE CO-ORDINATES IN UNITS OF THE SIXTH DECIMAL.

ARGUMENT XI.

Arg.	ξ'	Diff.	η'	Diff.	ζ'	Diff.	Arg.	ξ'	Diff.	η'	Diff.	ζ'	Diff.
0°	− 84	− 8	−120	+10	+ 1		180°	+ 37	+16	+156	− 3	− 1	
5	− 92	7	−110	10		+2	185	+ 53	15	+153	4		−2
10	− 99	6	−100	10	3		190	+ 68	16	+149	6	3	
15	−105	6	− 90	10		3	195	+ 84	15	+143	6		−3
20	−110	5	− 80	10	6		200	+ 99	15	+135	8	6	
25	−114	4	− 69	11		3	205	+114	13	+126	9		−3
30	−117	3	− 59	10	9		210	+127	13	+115	11	9	
35	−119	2	− 49	10		2	215	+140	11	+103	12		−2
40	−121	2	− 39	10	11		220	+151	10	+ 90	13	11	
45	−122	− 1	− 30	9		2	225	+161	8	+ 75	15		−2
50	−122	0	− 21	9	+13		230	+169	+ 6	+ 59	−17	−13	
55	−122	0	− 12	9		+1	235	+175	5	+ 42	18		−1
60	−122	0	− 3	9	14		240	+180	2	+ 24	18	14	
65	−122	+ 1	+ 6	8		+2	245	+182	0	+ 6	18		−2
70	−121	1	+ 14	8	16		250	+182	− 2	− 12	18	16	
75	−120	1	+ 22	8		0	255	+180	4	− 30	18		0
80	−119	1	+ 30	8	16		260	+176	6	− 48	18	16	
85	−118	2	+ 38	8		0	265	+170	7	− 66	16		0
90	−116	2	+ 46	8	16		270	+163	10	− 82	15	16	
95	−114	2	+ 54	+ 9		0	275	+153	11	− 97	14		0
100	−112	+ 3	+ 63	+ 8	+16		280	+142	−13	−111	−13	−16	
105	−109	4	+ 71	8		−1	285	+129	14	−124	11		+1
110	−105	4	+ 79	9	15		290	+115	14	−135	10	15	
115	−101	5	+ 88	8		−1	295	+101	16	−145	8		1
120	− 96	6	+ 96	8	14		300	+ 85	16	−153	6	14	
125	− 90	7	+104	8		−2	305	+ 69	16	−159	4		2
130	− 83	7	+112	8	12		310	+ 53	17	−163	2	12	
135	− 76	9	+120	8		−2	315	+ 36	16	−165	− 1		2
140	− 67	10	+128	7	10		320	+ 20	16	−166	+ 1	10	
145	− 57	+11	+135	6		−2	325	+ 4	15	−165	+ 3		2
150	− 46	+12	+141	+ 5	+ 8		330	− 11	−15	−162	+ 4	− 8	
155	− 34	13	+146	5		−3	335	− 26	14	−158	+ 6		+3
160	− 21	13	+151	3	5		340	− 40	12	−152	6	5	
165	− 8	15	+154	+ 2		−3	345	− 52	12	−146	6		3
170	+ 7	15	+156	0	+ 2		350	− 64	12	−138	8	− 2	
175	+ 22	15	+156	0		−3	355	− 74	10	−129	9		+3
180	+ 37	+10	+156		− 1		360	− 84	−10	−120	+ 9	+ 1	

TABLE IV. — *Continued.*

PERTURBATIONS OF THE CO-ORDINATES IN UNITS OF THE SIXTH DECIMAL.

ARGUMENT XII.						ARGUMENT XIII.					
Arg.	ξ'	Diff.	η'	Diff.	ζ'	Diff.	Arg.	ξ'	Diff.	η'	Diff.	ζ'	Diff.
0	+ 5	+20	+ 5	+12	+23	-8	0	+23	-2	-15	-3	-8	
10	25	19	17	11	15	9	10	21	2	18	3	7	
20	44	18	28	11	+ 6	9	20	19	3	21	3	6	
30	62	18	30	11	- 3	9	30	16	3	24	3	6	
40	78	16	48	9	12	9	40	13	4	27	3	5	
50	92	14	56	8	20	8	50	9	5	30	3	3	
60	104	12	61	5	28	8	60	+ 4	5	33	3	2	
70	112	8	65	4	35	7	70	- 1	6	35	-2	-1	
80	117	5	66	+1	41	6	80	7	7	35	0	+1	
90	118	+1	66	0	45	4	90	14	6	35	+2	2	
100	+116	-2	+63	-3	-40	4	100	-20	-6	-33	+4	+3	
110	110	-6	58	-5	51	-2	110	26	6	29	5	5	
120	100	10	52	6	51	0	120	32	5	24	6	6	
130	88	13	44	8	50	+1	130	37	3	18	8	6	
140	73	15	35	9	47	3	140	40	-2	10	8	7	
150	55	18	25	10	42	5	150	42	+1	- 2	9	8	
160	35	20	14	11	37	5	160	41	2	+ 7	8	8	
170	+ 15	20	+ 3	11	30	7	170	39	4	16	6	8	
180	- 6	21	- 7	10	23	7	180	35	5	24	7	8	
190	27	21	18	11	15	8	190	30	7	31	8	7	
200	- 47	20	-28	10	- 6	9	200	-23	+8	+36	+4	+6	
210	65	-18	37	-9	+ 3	+9	210	15	8	40	+1	6	
220	81	16	45	8	12	9	220	- 7	8	41	0	5	
230	95	14	52	7	20	8	230	+ 1	8	41	-1	3	
240	105	10	57	5	28	8	240	9	7	40	3	2	
250	113	8	61	4	35	7	250	16	5	37	5	+1	
260	116	3	63	-2	41	6	260	21	5	32	6	-1	
270	117	-1	63	0	45	4	270	26	3	26	5	2	
280	114	+3	62	+1	49	4	280	29	1	21	6	3	
290	107	7	59	3	51	+2	290	+30	+1	15	6	5	
300	- 97	10	-54	5	+51	0	300	+31	0	+ 9	-5	-6	
310	85	+12	47	+ 7	50	-1	310	31	-1	+ 4	5	6	
320	70	15	39	9	47	3	320	30	1	- 1	4	7	
330	53	17	29	10	42	5	330	29	2	5	3	8	
340	35	18	18	11	37	6	340	27	2	8	4	8	
350	- 15	20	- 7	11	30	7	350	25	-2	12	-3	8	
360	+ 5	+20	+ 5	+12	+23	-7	360	+23		-15		-8	

TABLE IV. — *Continued.*

PERTURBATIONS OF THE CO-ORDINATES IN UNITS OF THE SIXTH DECIMAL.

ARGUMENT XIV.

Arg.	ξ'	Diff.	η'	Diff.	ζ'	Diff.
0	-37	+3	-12	-5	+1	
10	34	3	17	6	1	
20	31	3	23	6	1	
30	27	4	28	6	1	
40	22	5	32	4	1	
50	16	6	35	3	+1	
60	10	6	38	3	0	
70	-3	7	39	-1	0	
80	+4	7	39	0	0	
90	11	7	38	+1	0	
		7		2		
100	+18	+6	-36	+4	0	
110	24	6	32	4	0	
120	30	4	28	6	0	
130	34	4	22	6	-1	
140	38	2	16	7	1	
150	40	+1	9	7	1	
160	41	0	-2	8	1	
170	41	-2	+6	7	1	
180	39	3	13	7	1	
190	36	4	20	6	1	
200	+32	-5	+26	+5	-1	
210	27	6	31	4	1	
220	21	7	35	3	1	
230	14	7	38	1	-1	
240	+7	7	39	+1	0	
250	0	7	40	-1	0	
260	-7	7	39	2	0	
270	14	6	37	3	0	
280	20	5	34	4	0	
290	25	6	30	5	0	
300	-30	-3	+25	-5	0	
310	33	3	20	6	+1	
320	36	2	14	7	1	
330	38	-1	7	6	1	
340	39	+1	+1	6	1	
350	38	+1	-5	-7	1	
360	-37		-12		+1	

ARGUMENT XV.

Arg.	ξ'	Diff.	η'	Diff.	ζ'	Diff.
0	-601	+81	+413	+97	+17	-2
10	520	97	510	83	15	3
20	423	111	593	64	12	3
30	312	119	657	44	9	3
40	193	125	701	23	5	4
50	-68	127	724	+1	+2	8
60	+59	127	725	-21	-2	4
70	184	125	704	42	6	4
80	304	120	662	63	9	8
90	415	111	599	80	12	3
		98		80		3
100	+513	+82	+519	-97	-15	-2
110	595	86	422	109	17	2
120	660	66	313	119	19	1
130	704	44	194	135	20	-1
140	727	23	+69	127	21	0
150	728	+1	-58	126	21	+1
160	707	-21	183	116	20	1
170	664	-63	302	-111	19	+2
180	+601		-413		-17	

ARGUMENT XVI.

Arg.	ξ'	Diff.	η'	Diff.	ζ'	Diff.
0	+239	-57	+301	+36	-5	
10	182	62	337	26	4	
20	120	66	363	15	3	
30	+54	66	378	+4	2	
40	-14	68	382	-8	-1	
50	81	67	374	20	+1	
60	146	65	354	30	2	
70	206	60	324	40	3	
80	260	54	284	49	4	
90	306	46	235	56	5	
		87		66		
100	-343	-26	+179	-61	+6	
110	369	15	118	65	6	
120	384	-4	+53	68	7	
130	388	+8	-13	66	7	
140	380	20	79	64	7	
150	360	31	143	59	7	
160	329	41	202	53	6	
170	288	+49	255	-46	6	
180	-239		-301		+5	

From the Arguments >180° subtract 180°, and reverse the sign of ξ', η', and ζ'.

TABLE IV. — *Continued.*

PERTURBATIONS OF THE CO-ORDINATES IN UNITS OF THE SIXTH DECIMAL.

ARGUMENT XVII. / ARGUMENT XIX.

Arg.	ξ'	Diff.	η'	Diff.	ζ'	Diff.	Arg.	ξ'	Diff.	η'	Diff.	ζ'	Diff.
0	-252	+8	+19	+43	+1		0	+172	-6	-25	-30	-4	
10	244	14	62	41	0		10	166	12	55	28	4	
20	230	22	103	38	-1		20	154	16	83	26	4	
30	209	28	141	34	2		30	138	20	109	22	3	
40	180	33	175	29	3		40	118	24	131	19	3	
50	147	38	204	22	4		50	94	27	150	14	2	
60	109	41	226	16	4		60	67	29	164	9	2	
70	68	44	242	+8	5		70	38	30	173	-4	1	
80	-21	44	250	0	5		80	+8	30	177	+2	-1	
90	+20	43	250	-7	6		90	-22	29	175	7	+0	
100	+63	+42	+243	-15	-6		100	-51	-28	-168	+12	+1	
110	105	38	228	21	6		110	79	26	156	17	1	
120	143	34	207	29	6		120	105	22	130	21	2	
130	177	28	179	33	5		130	127	19	118	24	2	
140	205	23	146	37	5		140	146	14	94	28	3	
150	228	15	109	41	4		150	160	9	66	29	3	
160	243	8	68	43	3		160	169	-4	37	31	4	
170	251	+1	+25	-44	2		170	173	+1	-6	+31	4	
180	+252		-19		-1		180	-172		+25		+4	

ARGUMENT XVIII. / ARGUMENT XX.

Arg.	ξ'	Diff.	η'	Diff.	ζ'	Diff.	Arg.	ξ'	Diff.	η'	Diff.	ζ'	Diff.
0	+110	+16	+36	-10	+3		0	-120	+1	-65	-20	+4	+8
10	126	13	26	12	+1		10	128	4	85	17	12	8
20	138	8	14	11	-1		20	124	8	102	14	20	7
30	146	+3	+3	12	3		30	116	12	116	10	27	6
40	149	-1	-9	12	5		40	104	14	126	7	33	5
50	148	6	21	10	6		50	90	18	133	-2	38	4
60	143	10	31	10	8		60	72	19	135	+1	42	3
70	133	14	41	9	9		70	53	22	134	6	45	+1
80	119	17	50	7	10		80	31	22	128	9	46	0
90	102	21	57	5	11		90	-9	22	119	13	46	-1
100	+81	-23	-62	-4	-11		100	+13	+22	-106	+17	+45	-3
110	58	25	66	-2	11		110	35	22	89	19	42	4
120	33	26	68	+1	10		120	57	19	70	21	38	5
130	+7	26	67	3	10		130	76	17	40	22	33	7
140	-19	26	64	4	9		140	93	14	27	24	26	7
150	44	24	60	7	·7		150	107	11	-3	23	19	7
160	69	22	53	8	6		160	118	7	+20	23	12	8
170	90	-20	45	+9	4		170	125	+3	43	+22	+4	-8
180	-110		-36		-3		180	+120		+65		-4	

From the Arguments >180° subtract 180°, and reverse the sign of ξ', η', and ζ'.

TABLE IV. — *Continued.*
PERTURBATIONS OF THE CO–ORDINATES IN UNITS OF THE SIXTH DECIMAL.

ARGUMENT XXI.

Arg.	ξ'	Diff.	η'	Diff.	ζ'	Diff.
0	+ 62		+ 70		−1	
		−15		+ 9		
10	47		88	7	−1	
20	31	16	95	7	0	
30	+ 14	17	99	4	0	
40	− 4	18	100	+ 1	0	
50	21	17	98	− 2	0	
60	38	17	93	5	0	
70	54	16	85	8	0	
80	68	14	74	11	+1	
90	80	12	61	13	1	
		9		16		
100	− 89	− 7	+ 46	−16	+1	
110	96	4	30	17	1	
120	100	− 1	+ 13	17	1	
130	101	+ 3	− 4	17	1	
140	96	5	21	17	1	
150	93	8	38	15	1	
160	85	10	53	14	1	
170	75	+13	67	−19	1	
180	− 62		− 79		+1	

ARGUMENT XXIII.

Arg.	ξ'	Diff.	η'	Diff.	ζ'	Diff.
0	−53		+ 4		0	
		+ 1		+ 9		
10	52		13	9	0	
20	49	3	22	9	0	
30	44	5	30	8	0	
40	36	6	37	7	0	
50	31	7	44	7	−1	
60	23	8	49	5	1	
70	15	8	52	3	1	
80	− 6	9	54	+ 2	1	
90	+ 4	10	54	0	1	
		9		− 2		
100	+13	+ 9	+52	− 3	−1	
110	22	8	40	4	1	
120	30	8	45	6	1	
130	37	7	39	6	−1	
140	43	8	32	7	0	
150	48	5	24	8	0	
160	51	+ 2	15	9	0	
170	53	0	+ 6	0	0	
180	+53		− 4	−10	0	

ARGUMENT XXII.

Arg.	ξ'	Diff.	η'	Diff.	ζ'	Diff.
0	+79		+50		0	
		−10		+13		
10	69		63	11	0	
20	57	12	74	9	0	
30	43	14	83	6	0	
40	28	15	80	+ 4	0	
50	+12	16	93	0	0	
60	− 4	16	93	− 2	0	
70	20	16	91	5	0	
80	36	16	86	7	0	
90	50	14	79	10	0	
		13		10		
100	−63	−11	+69	−12	0	
110	74	9	57	14	0	
120	83	5	43	15	0	
130	89	4	29	16	0	
140	93	− 1	+12	16	0	
150	94	+ 3	− 4	16	0	
160	91	5	20	16	0	
170	86	+ 7	36	−14	0	
180	−79		−50		0	

ARGUMENT XXIV.

Arg.	ξ'	Diff.	η'	Diff.	ζ'	Diff.
0	−53		+32		+2	
		+ 1		− 8		
10	52		24	9	+1	
20	49	3	15	9	0	
30	45	4	+ 6	9	−1	
40	39	8	− 4	10	1	
50	32	7	13	9	2	
60	24	8	22	8	3	
70	16	8	30	8	4	
80	− 6	10	36	8	5	
90	+ 3	9	44	6	5	
		9		6		
100	+12	+ 9	−49	− 3	−5	
110	21	6	52	2	6	
120	20	6	54	0	6	
130	36	7	54	+ 1	5	
140	42	6	53	3	5	
150	47	5	50	3	5	
160	51	4	45	6	4	
170	53	+ 2	39	+ 7	3	
180	+53	0	−32		−2	

From the Arguments >180° subtract 180°, and reverse the sign of ξ', η', and ζ'.

TABLE IV. — *Continued.*

PERTURBATIONS OF THE CO-ORDINATES IN UNITS OF THE SIXTH DECIMAL.

ARGUMENT XXV.

Arg.	ξ'	Diff.	η'	Diff.	ζ'	Diff.
0	+27	−10	−11	−6	0	
10	17		16		0	
20	+7	10	20	4	0	
30	−3	10	24	4	0	
40	14	11	27	3	0	
50	24	10	29	2	0	
60	33	9	30	−1	0	
70	41	8	03	0	0	
80	48	7	30	0	0	
90	54	6	28	+2	0	
100	−58	4	−26	2	0	
110	60	−2	23	+3	0	
120	60	0	19	4	0	
130	58	+2	14	5	0	
140	55	3	9	5	0	
150	50	3	−4	5	0	
160	44	6	+1	5	0	
170	36	6	6	5	0	
180	−27	+0	+11	+6	0	

ARGUMENT XXVII.

Arg.	ξ'	Diff.	η'	Diff.	ζ'	Diff.
0	−25	+4	+17	+4	0	
10	21		21		0	
20	17	4	25	4	0	
30	13	4	27	2	0	
40	8	6	29	2	0	
50	−3	5	30	+1	0	
60	+2	5	30	0	0	
70	7	5	29	−1	0	
80	12	5	27	2	0	
90	17	5	25	2	0	
100	+21	4	+21	4	0	
110	24	+3	17	−4	0	
120	27	3	13	4	0	
130	29	2	8	6	0	
140	30	+1	+3	5	0	
150	30	0	−2	5	0	
160	29	−1	7	6	0	
170	27	2	12	5	0	
180	+25	−2	−17	−6	0	

ARGUMENT XXVI.

Arg.	ξ'	Diff.	η'	Diff.	ζ'	Diff.
0	+29	−4	−21	−4	0	
10	25		25		0	
20	21	4	28	3	0	
30	16	5	31	3	0	
40	11	6	33	2	0	
50	+5	6	34	−1	0	
60	−1	6	33	+1	0	
70	7	6	32	1	0	
80	13	6	30	2	0	
90	18	5	26	4	0	
100	−23	6	−22	4	0	
110	27	−4	18	+4	0	
120	30	3	13	5	0	
130	32	2	7	6	0	
140	33	1	−1	6	0	
150	34	−1	+5	6	0	
160	33	+1	11	6	0	
170	32	1	16	5	0	
180	−29	+2	+21	+5	0	

ARGUMENT XXVIII.

Arg.	ξ'	Diff.	η'	Diff.	ζ'	Diff.
0	+14	−1	−3	+6	0	
10	13		+3		0	
20	12	1	8	5	0	
30	11	1	13	5	0	
40	9	2	18	5	0	
50	7	2	22	4	0	
60	5	2	26	4	0	
70	+3	2	29	3	0	
80	0	3	31	2	0	
90	−2	2	32	+1	0	
100	−5	3	+32	0	0	
110	7	−2	31	−1	0	
120	9	2	29	2	0	
130	11	2	26	3	0	
140	12	1	23	3	0	
150	13	1	18	5	0	
160	14	−1	13	5	0	
170	14	0	8	5	0	
180	−14	0	+3	−6	0	

From the Arguments >180° subtract 180°, and reverse the sign of ξ', η', and ζ'.

TABLE IV. — *Continued.*

PERTURBATIONS OF THE CO-ORDINATES IN UNITS OF THE SIXTH DECIMAL.

ARGUMENT XXIX.

Arg.	ξ'	Diff.	η'	Diff.	ζ'
0	+19		-5		0
10	17	-2	4		0
20	14	3	3		0
30	11	3	2		0
40	7	4	-1		0
50	+4	3	+1		0
60	0	4	2		0
70	-4	4	3		0
80	8	4	4		0
90	11	3	5		0
100	-14	3	+6		0
110	17	-3	7		0
120	19	2	7		0
130	21	2	7		0
140	22	-1	7		0
150	22	0	7		0
160	22	0	7		0
170	21	+1	6		0
180	-19	+2	+5		0

ARGUMENT XXX.

Arg.	ξ'	Diff.	η'	Diff.	ζ'
0	-9		-9		-2
10	7		12		3
20	5		15		3
30	-2		17		2
40	0		18		2
50	+3		19		2
60	5		20		2
70	8		20		1
80	10		19		1
90	12		18		-1
100	+13		-16		0
110	14		14		+1
120	15		11		1
130	15		8		1
140	15		5		2
150	14		-1		2
160	13		+2		2
170	11		6		2
180	+9		+9		+2

ARGUMENT XXXI.

Arg.	ξ'	η'	ζ'
0	-9	-3	0
20	8	6	0
40	5	8	0
60	-2	10	0
80	+1	10	0
100	4	9	0
120	7	6	0
140	9	-3	0
160	10	0	0
180	+9	+3	0

ARGUMENT XXXII.

Arg.	ξ'	η'	ζ'
0	-8	+4	0
20	6	7	0
40	-4	9	0
60	0	10	0
80	+3	9	0
100	6	8	0
120	8	5	0
140	9	+2	0
160	9	-1	0
180	+8	-4	0

ARGUMENT XXXIII.

Arg.	ξ'	η'	ζ'
0	+2	-10	0
20	5	8	0
40	8	6	-1
60	9	-3	1
80	10	0	1
100	9	+4	1
120	8	7	1
140	5	9	-1
160	+2	10	0
180	-2	+10	0

ARGUMENT XXXIV.

Arg.	ξ'	η'	ζ'
0	-7	-1	0
20	7	+1	0
40	7	4	0
60	6	5	0
80	4	7	0
100	-1	7	0
120	+1	7	0
140	4	6	0
160	6	4	0
180	-7	+1	0

ARGUMENT XXXV.

Arg.	ξ'	η'	ζ'
0	+4	+5	0
20	+2	5	0
40	0	6	0
60	-2	5	0
80	4	4	0
100	5	3	0
120	6	+1	0
140	6	-1	0
160	5	3	0
180	-4	-5	0

ARGUMENT XXXVI.

Arg.	ξ'	η'	ζ'
0	-4	+3	0
20	-1	+1	-1
40	+2	-1	1
60	4	3	2
80	7	5	2
100	8	6	2
120	9	6	2
140	8	5	1
160	6	4	-1
180	+4	-3	0

ARGUMENT XXXVII.

Arg.	ξ'	η'	ζ'
0	+3	-4	0
20	+1	5	0
40	-1	5	0
60	2	5	0
80	4	4	0
100	5	2	0
120	6	-1	0
140	5	+1	0
160	4	3	0
180	-3	+4	0

ARGUMENT XXXVIII.

Arg.	ξ'	η'	ζ'
0	+4	-5	-1
20	2	6	1
40	+1	6	-1
60	-1	6	0
80	3	5	0
100	5	4	0
120	6	-2	0
140	6	+1	+1
160	5	3	1
180	-4	+5	+1

From the Arguments $>180°$ subtract $180°$, and reverse the sign of ξ', η', and ζ'.

TABLE IV. — *Concluded.*
PERTURBATIONS OF THE CO-ORDINATES IN UNITS OF THE SIXTH DECIMAL.

ARGUMENT XXXIX.

Arg.	ξ'	η'	ζ'
0	+4	+3	0
20	3	4	0
40	+2	5	0
60	.0	5	0
80	-2	5	0
100	3	4	0
120	5	2	0
140	5	+1	0
160	5	-1	0
180	-4	-3	0

ARGUMENT XLIII.

Arg.	ξ'	η'	ζ'
0	-3	0	0
20	2	+1	0
40	2	1	0
60	1	2	0
80	-1	2	0
100	+1	2	0
120	1	2	0
140	2	1	0
160	2	+1	0
180	+3	0	0

ARGUMENT XLVII.

Arg.	ξ'	η'	ζ'
0	+1	+1	0
20	0	1	0
40	0	1	0
60	0	1	0
80	-1	+1	0
100	1	0	0
120	1	0	0
140	1	0	0
160	1	-1	0
180	-1	-1	0

ARGUMENT XL.

Arg.	ξ'	η'	ζ'
0	-3	-6	+1
20	3	5	1
40	2	4	1
60	2	-2	1
80	-1	0	1
100	+1	+2	1
120	2	4	+1
140	2	5	0
160	3	6	0
180	+3	+6	-1

ARGUMENT XLIV.

Arg.	ξ'	η'	ζ'
0	-3	+1	0
20	3	0	0
40	2	-1	0
60	2	2	0
80	-1	3	0
100	0	3	0
120	+1	3	0
140	2	3	0
160	2	2	0
180	+3	-1	0

ARGUMENT XLVIII.

Arg.	ξ'	η'	ζ'
0	0	-1	0
20	0	1	0
40	0	1	0
60	-1	1	0
80	1	1	0
100	1	-1	0
120	1	0	0
140	1	0	0
160	-1	+1	0
180	0	+1	0

ARGUMENT XLI.

Arg.	ξ'	η'	ζ'
0	+4	+1	0
20	3	1	0
40	2	1	0
60	+1	1	0
80	0	1	0
100	-1	+1	0
120	3	0	0
140	3	0	0
160	4	-1	0
180	-4	-1	0

ARGUMENT XLV.

Arg.	ξ'	η'	ζ'
0	-2	-1	0
20	2	0	0
40	2	0	0
60	2	+1	0
80	1	1	0
100	-1	2	0
120	0	2	0
140	+1	2	0
160	2	1	0
180	+2	+1	0

ARGUMENT XLIX.

Arg.	ξ'	η'	ζ'
0	+1	0	0
20	1	0	0
40	1	-1	0
60	+1	1	0
80	0	1	0
100	0	1	0
120	-1	1	0
140	1	-1	0
160	1	0	0
180	-1	0	0

ARGUMENT XLII.

Arg.	ξ'	η'	ζ'
0	-2	-1	0
20	2	1	0
40	-1	2	0
60	0	2	0
80	0	2	0
100	+1	2	0
120	2	2	0
140	2	-1	0
160	2	0	0
180	+2	+1	0

ARGUMENT XLVI.

Arg.	ξ'	η'	ζ'
0	0	+1	0
20	0	+1	0
40	+1	0	0
60	1	0	0
80	2	-1	0
100	2	1	0
120	2	1	0
140	2	1	0
160	+1	1	0
180	0	-1	0

From the Arguments >180° subtract 180°, and reverse the sign of ξ', η', and ζ'.

TABLE V.

LOGARITHMS FOR REFERRING THE PERTURBATIONS TO THE EQUATOR.

Mean Equinox of the beginning of the Year.

Years.	$\cos(x_1 x)$	$\cos(y_1 x)$	$\cos(z_1 x)$	$\cos(x_1 y)$	$\cos(y_1 y)$	$\cos(z_1 y)$	$\cos(x_1 z)$	$\cos(y_1 z)$	$\cos(z_1 z)$
1851	9.937163	9.667863n	9.269727n	9.531058	9.912469	9.667602n	9.566586	9.530572	9.937239
1852B	9.937107	9.668063n	9.269685n	9.531305	9.912414	9.667639n	9.566685	9.530509	9.937231
1853	9.937051	9.668264n	9.269643n	9.531552	9.912360	9.667674n	9.566785	9.530447	9.937222
1854	9.936995	9.668464n	9.269601n	9.531799	9.912305	9.667710n	9.566884	9.530384	9.937214
1855	9.936939	9.668665n	9.269559n	9.532046	9.912250	9.667746n	9.566983	9.530323	9.937205
1856B	9.936882	9.668865n	9.269516n	9.532293	9.912195	9.667782n	9.567082	9.530259	9.937197
1857	9.936826	9.669065n	9.269474n	9.532540	9.912141	9.667818n	9.567181	9.530197	9.937188
1858	9.936769	9.669265n	9.269432n	9.532786	9.912086	9.667854n	9.567280	9.530134	9.937180
1859	9.936713	9.669465n	9.269390n	9.533033	9.912031	9.667890n	9.567379	9.530072	9.937171
1860B	9.936656	9.669665n	9.269347n	9.533279	9.911976	9.667925n	9.567478	9.530009	9.937163
1861	9.936600	9.669865n	9.269305n	9.533525	9.911922	9.667961n	9.567577	9.529947	9.937154
1862	9.936543	9.670061n	9.269262n	9.533771	9.911867	9.667997n	9.567676	9.529884	9.937146
1863	9.936487	9.670264n	9.269220n	9.534017	9.911812	9.668033n	9.567775	9.529821	9.937137
1864B	9.936430	9.670463n	9.269177n	9.534263	9.911757	9.668069n	9.567873	9.529758	9.937129
1865	9.936374	9.670663n	9.269135n	9.534509	9.911703	9.668105n	9.567973	9.529796	9.937120
1866	9.936317	9.670862n	9.269092n	9.534754	9.911648	9.668141n	9.568072	9.529633	9.937112
1867	9.936261	9.671061n	9.269049n	9.534999	9.911593	9.668177n	9.568170	9.529570	9.937104
1868B	9.936204	9.671260n	9.269006n	9.535244	9.911538	9.668212n	9.568268	9.529507	9.937096
1869	9.936148	9.671459n	9.268964n	9.535489	9.911484	9.668248n	9.568367	9.529444	9.937087
1870	9.936091	9.671657n	9.268921n	9.535734	9.911429	9.668284n	9.568465	9.529381	9.937079
1871	9.936034	9.671856n	9.268878n	9.535979	9.911374	9.668320n	9.568564	9.529318	9.937070
1872B	9.935977	9.672054n	9.268835n	9.536223	9.911319	9.668355n	9.568662	9.529255	9.937062
1873	9.935921	9.672253n	9.268792n	9.536467	9.911264	9.668391n	9.568761	9.529192	9.937053
1874	9.935864	9.672451n	9.268749n	9.536711	9.911209	9.668426n	9.568859	9.529129	9.937045
1875	9.935807	9.672649n	9.268706n	9.536955	9.911154	9.668462n	9.568957	9.529066	9.937037
1876B	9.935750	9.672847n	9.268663n	9.537199	9.911099	9.668497n	9.569055	9.529002	9.937029
1877	9.935694	9.673045n	9.268620n	9.537473	9.911044	9.668533n	9.569153	9.528939	9.937020
1878	9.935637	9.673243n	9.268577n	9.537686	9.910989	9.668569n	9.569251	9.528875	9.937012
1879	9.935580	9.673441n	9.268534n	9.537929	9.910934	9.668605n	9.569349	9.528812	9.937004
1880B	9.935523	9.673638n	9.268491n	9.538172	9.910879	9.668640n	9.569447	9.528748	9.936996
1881	9.935466	9.673836n	9.268448n	9.538415	9.910824	9.668676n	9.569545	9.528685	9.936987
1882	9.935499	9.674033n	9.268405n	9.538658	9.910769	9.668711n	9.569643	9.528621	9.936979
1883	9.935352	9.674230n	9.268362n	9.538901	9.910714	9.668747n	9.569741	9.528558	9.936971
1884B	9.935295	9.674427n	9.268318n	9.539143	9.910658	9.668782n	9.569839	9.528494	9.936963
1885	9.935223	9.674624n	9.268275n	9.539385	9.910603	9.668818n	9.569937	9.528431	9.936954
1886	9.935161	9.674821n	9.268232n	9.539627	9.910547	9.668854n	9.570035	9.528367	9.936946
1887	9.935114	9.675018n	9.268189n	9.539869	9.910492	9.668890n	9.570133	9.528303	9.936937
1888B	9.935066	9.675214n	9.268145n	9.540110	9.910436	9.668925n	9.570230	9.528239	9.936929
1889	9.935009	9.675411n	9.268102n	9.540352	9.910381	9.668961n	9.570328	9.528176	9.936920
1890	9.934951	9.675607n	9.268059n	9.540593	9.910325	9.668996n	9.570426	9.528112	9.936912
1891	9.934894	9.675803n	9.268016n	9.540834	9.910270	9.669032n	9.570524	9.528048	9.936904
1892B	9.934836	9.675999n	9.267972n	9.541075	9.910214	9.669067n	9.570621	9.527984	9.936896
1893	9.934779	9.676195n	9.267929n	9.541316	9.910159	9.669103n	9.570719	9.527921	9.936887
1894	9.934721	9.676391n	9.267885n	9.541556	9.910103	9.669138n	9.570817	9.527857	9.936879
1895	9.934663	9.676587n	9.267842n	9.541796	9.910047	9.669174n	9.570915	9.527793	9.936871
1896B	9.934605	9.676782n	9.267798n	9.542036	9.909991	9.669209n	9.571012	9.527729	9.936863
1897	9.934548	9.676978n	9.267755n	9.542276	9.909936	9.669245n	9.571110	9.527665	9.936854
1898	9.934490	9.677173n	9.267711n	9.542516	9.909880	9.669280n	9.571207	9.527601	9.936846
1899	9.934432	9.677369n	9.267667n	9.542756	9.909824	9.669316n	9.571305	9.527537	9.936838
1900B	9.934374	9.677564n	9.267693n	9.542995	9.909768	9.669351n	9.571402	9.527473	9.936830

TABLE VI.

VARIATIONS OF THE LOGARITHMS IN UNITS OF THE SIXTH DECIMAL
BY VARYING Ω AND ϵ.

$\Delta \Omega$	$\Delta \cos (x_1 x)$	$\Delta \cos (y_1 x)$	$\Delta \cos (z_1 x)$	$\Delta \cos (x_1 y)$	$\Delta \cos (y_1 y)$	$\Delta \cos (z_1 y)$	$\Delta \cos (x_1 z)$	$\Delta \cos (y_1 z)$	$\Delta \cos (z_1 z)$
1	− 1.0	+ 4.0	−1.0	+ 4.9	− 1.1	+0.8	+ 2.0	− 1.1	−0.2
2	2.1	8.0	1.9	9.9	2.1	1.5	3.9	2.2	0.3
3	3.1	12.0	2.9	14.8	3.2	2.3	5.9	3.3	0.5
4	4.1	16.0	3.9	19.7	4.3	3.1	7.9	4.4	0.7
5	5.1	20.0	4.8	24.6	5.3	3.8	9.8	5.5	0.8
6	6.2	24.0	5.8	29.6	6.4	4.6	11.8	6.6	1.0
7	7.2	28.0	6.8	34.5	7.5	5.4	13.8	7.7	1.2
8	8.2	32.0	7.8	39.4	8.6	6.2	15.8	8.8	1.4
9	9.3	36.0	8.7	44.4	9.6	6.9	17.7	9.9	1.5
10	−10.3	+40.0	−9.7	+49.3	−10.7	+7.7	+19.7	−10.1	−1.7

$\Delta \epsilon$	$\Delta \cos (x_1 x)$	$\Delta \cos (y_1 x)$	$\Delta \cos (z_1 x)$	$\Delta \cos (x_1 y)$	$\Delta \cos (y_1 y)$	$\Delta \cos (z_1 y)$	$\Delta \cos (x_1 z)$	$\Delta \cos (y_1 z)$	$\Delta \cos (z_1 z)$
1				− 2.0	− 1.3	+ 3.8	+ 2.0	+ 5.0	− 1.0
2				4.0	2.6	7.6	4.0	10.0	2.0
3				6.0	3.9	11.4	6.0	15.0	3.0
4				8.0	5.2	15.2	8.0	20.0	4.0
5				10.0	6.5	19.0	10.0	25.0	5.0
6				12.0	7.8	22.8	12.0	30.0	6.0
7				14.0	9.1	26.6	14.0	35.0	7.0
8				16.0	10.4	30.4	16.0	40.0	8.0
9				18.0	11.7	34.2	18.0	45.0	9.0
10				−20.0	−13.0	+38.0	+20.0	+50.0	−10.0

TABLE VII.

CONSTANTS FOR THE EQUATOR.

Equator and mean Equinox at the beginning of the Year.

Years.	A'	B'	C'	log sin a.	log sin b.	log sin c.
	° ′ ″	° ′ ″	° ′ ″			
1851	118 16 32.4	22 33 50.1	47 22 22.8	9.992347	9.947054	9.699841
1852B	118 17 23.5	22 34 41.1	47 23 1.2	9.992348	9.940044	9.699866
1853	118 18 14.3	22 35 31.8	47 23 39.3	9.992350	9.940034	9.699801
1854	118 19 5.1	22 36 22.5	47 24 17.5	9.992351	9.940024	9.699916
1855	118 19 56.0	22 37 13.3	47 24 55.6	9.992353	9.940014	9.699941
1856B	118 20 47.1	22 38 4.3	47 25 34.0	9.992354	9.947004	9.699966
1857	118 21 37.9	22 38 55.0	47 26 12.1	9.992356	9.946994	9.699901
1858	118 22 28.7	22 39 45.7	47 26 50.3	9.992357	9.946984	9.700016
1859	118 23 19.6	22 40 36.5	47 27 28.4	9.992359	9.946974	9.700041
1860B	118 24 10.7	22 41 27.5	47 28 6.8	9.992360	9.946965	9.700066
1861	118 25 1.5	22 42 19.2	47 28 44.9	9.992362	9.946955	9.700001
1862	118 25 52.3	22 43 8.9	47 29 23.1	9.992364	9.946945	9.700116
1863	118 26 43.1	22 43 59.7	47 30 1.2	9.992366	9.946935	9.700141
1864B	118 27 34.2	22 44 50.8	47 30 39.6	9.992367	9.946926	9.700166
1865	118 28 25.1	22 45 41.5	47 31 17.7	9.992369	9.946916	9.700191
1866	118 29 15.9	22 46 32.3	47 31 55.9	9.992370	9.946906	9.700216
1867	118 30 6.8	22 47 23.1	47 32 34.0	9.992372	9.946896	9.700241
1868B	118 30 57.9	22 48 14.2	47 33 12.3	9.992373	9.946887	9.700266
1869	118 31 48.7	22 49 4.9	47 33 50.4	9.992375	9.946877	9.700291
1870	118 32 39.5	22 49 55.7	47 34 28.6	9.992377	9.946867	9.700316
1871	118 33 30.4	22 50 46.6	47 35 6.7	9.992379	9.946857	9.700341
1872B	118 34 21.6	22 51 37.7	47 35 45.0	9.992380	9.946847	9.700366
1873	118 35 12.4	22 52 48.4	47 36 23.1	9.992382	9.946837	9.700391
1874	118 36 3.2	22 53 19.2	47 37 1.3	9.992383	9.946827	9.700416
1875	118 36 54.1	22 54 10.1	47 37 39.4	9.992385	9.946817	9.700441
1876B	118 37 45.3	22 55 1.2	47 38 17.7	9.992386	9.946807	9.700465
1877	118 38 36.1	22 55 51.9	47 38 55.8	9.992388	9.946797	9.700490
1878	118 39 26.9	22 56 42.7	47 39 34.0	9.992389	9.946787	9.700515
1879	118 40 17.8	22 57 33.6	47 40 12.1	9.992391	9.946777	9.700540
1880B	118 41 8.9	22 58 24.7	47 40 50.5	9.992392	9.946767	9.700565
1881	118 41 59.7	22 59 15.4	47 41 28.6	9.992394	9.946757	9.700590
1882	118 42 50.5	23 0 6.2	47 42 6.8	9.992395	9.946747	9.700615
1883	118 43 41.4	23 0 57.1	47 42 44.9	9.992397	9.946737	9.700640
1884B	118 44 32.6	23 1 48.2	47 43 23.3	9.992398	9.946727	9.700664
1885	118 45 23.4	23 2 38.9	47 44 1.4	9.992400	9.946717	9.700689
1886	118 46 14.2	23 3 29.7	47 44 39.6	9.992401	9.946707	9.700714
1887	118 47 5.1	23 4 20.6	47 45 17.7	9.992403	9.946697	9.700739
1888B	118 47 56.2	23 5 11.7	47 45 56.0	9.992404	9.946687	9.700763
1889	118 48 47.0	23 6 2.4	47 46 34.1	9.992406	9.946677	9.700788
1890	118 49 37.8	23 6 53.2	47 47 12.2	9.992407	9.946667	9.700813
1891	118 50 28.7	23 7 44.1	47 47 50.3	9.992409	9.946657	9.700838
1892B	118 51 19.9	23 8 35.2	47 48 28.7	9.992410	9.946648	9.700862
1893	118 52 10.7	23 9 26.0	47 49 6.7	9.992412	9.946638	9.700887
1894	118 53 1.5	23 10 16.8	47 49 44.9	9.992413	9.946628	9.700912
1895	118 53 52.4	23 11 7.7	47 50 23.0	9.992415	9.946618	9.700937
1896B	118 54 43.6	23 11 58.8	47 51 1.4	9.992416	9.946608	9.700962
1897	118 55 34.4	23 12 49.6	47 51 39.5	9.992418	9.946598	9.700987
1898	118 56 25.2	23 13 40.4	47 52 17.7	9.992419	9.946588	9.701012
1899	118 57 16.1	23 14 31.3	47 52 55.8	9.992421	9.946578	9.701037
1900B	118 58 7.3	23 15 22.4	47 53 34.1	9.992422	9.946560	9.701061

TABLE VIII.

VARIATIONS OF THE CONSTANTS BY VARYING Ω AND e.

Δ Ω.	Δ A'	Δ B'	Δ C'	Δ log sin a.	Δ log sin b.	Δ log sin c.
1	+ 1.0	+ 1.0	+0.7	+0.0	−0.2	+0.5
2	2.0	2.0	1.5	0.1	0.4	1.1
3	3.0	3.0	2.2	0.1	0.6	1.6
4	4.0	4.0	2.9	0.1	0.8	2.1
5	5.0	5.0	3.7	0.1	1.0	2.6
6	6.0	6.0	4.4	0.2	1.2	3.2
7	7.0	7.0	5.1	0.2	1.4	3.7
8	8.0	8.1	5.9	0.2	1.6	4.2
9	9.0	9.1	6.6	0.3	1.8	4.8
10	+10.0	+10.1	+7.3	+0.3	−2.0	+5.3

Δ e.	Δ A'	Δ B'	Δ C'	Δ log sin a.	Δ log sin b.	Δ log sin c.
1		−0.2	−0.7		− 1.0	+ 3.0
2		0.4	1.5		2.0	6.0
3		0.6	2.2		3.0	9.0
4		0.8	2.9		4.0	12.0
5		1.0	3.6		5.0	15.0
6		1.3	4.4		6.0	18.0
7		1.5	5.1		7.0	21.0
8		1.7	5.8		8.0	24.0
9		1.9	6.6		9.0	27.0
10		−2.1	−7.3		−10.0	+30.0